Jack Palance: "Do you know what the secret of life is? One thing. Just one thing. You stick to that and everything else don't mean shit."
Billy Crystal: "Yeah, but what's that one thing?"
Jack Palance: "That's what you've got to figure out."
~From the movie *City Slickers*

Prologue

Okay, so what is this book about? First, let me say, do not be confused by the title of this book. I am in no way encouraging people to drink their problems away. It is a metaphor, which I will explain shortly.

Before I get to that though, allow me to tell you what this book is about. I mention growing up with disabilities, but this book is not a self-help book for disabled people. If that is what you are interested in I suggest you read Doctor

Phil or any other pop-psychology book. Personally I don't think it is logical or fair for anyone to suggest that their advice or thinking is a catchall that works for all people. Although Dr. Phil did have some good insights, one in particular I will point out in a later chapter. I have a found pop-psychology books disillusioning ever since I found out John Gray the author of Men Are From Mars Women are From Venus had been divorced 3 times. Well I guess he knows what not to do.

As of January of last year I suffered a stroke, and I do discuss that in this book, but make no mistake; this is not a book on how to deal with having a stroke. Nor is this book about how to deal with tragedy. There have been a number of books written about life after stroke and there have been a number of books written about dealing with tragedy. I am not qualified to counsel you on either of these subjects. If you are looking for religious explanations I suggest you read Why Bad Things Happen To Good People by Rabbi Harold S. Kushner.

I explore some of the absurdities and contradictions that exist in our culture. I think I do a pretty good job of it to, but that is not the focus of this book

either. There is a fantastic book called
Shock Treatment by Karen Finley that
does a much more in-depth, analysis of
contemporary American Culture then I
could ever offer you.

So now that I have told you what
not to expect. Let me explain what this
book does entail. Basically this book is my
life's story. I give opinions on a variety of
subjects as it pertains to me. I give tid-
bits of advice, when appropriate, but be
advised, my advice may not fit everyone.
I have learned a lot from mistakes I have
made during my life. I certainly think I
could have dealt better with my disability
growing up. If I had to go through it
again, would I do things differently?
Certainly, I think anyone who claims to
have never made a mistake in their life is
either in denial or just a pompous ass.

I have never been politically correct
unless I had to be, so don't expect politi-
cal correctness in this book. I don't sugar
coat anything, I tell things the way I see
them. With maybe a touch of, dare I say
it humor added (if you couldn't tell that
by the title of my book). I say that with a
touch of sarcasm because the general
opinion is when you are speaking of disabilities you must be serious. I don't

know who wrote that rule but I think it
sucks. I will agree many of the "jokes"
made of disabled people are cruel and
insensitive, however they depend on who
is telling them, the setting in which they
are being told, and the intent of the person telling it. I.E If a comedian in a come-
dy club makes a joke involving blind people, that doesn't offend me. However, if a
coworker I hardly know is telling the same
joke in a work setting, I feel that is inappropriate. I still think having a sense of
humor is so important and I will explain
why in a later chapter. Lets just say, if I
didn't have a sense of humor about my
life and the things that have happened to
me, I could not possibly deal with the
emotional stress that comes with being
disabled.
So to sum up, if you are one who gets
easily offended, I suggest you close this
book and read no further than this. I
don't want any hate mail. With that in
mind, I will continue.

I'll have you know I considered many
titles for this book before I finally decided
on "_When Life Gives You Lemons, Add
Tequila And Salt'. First I thought of
Climbing obstacles, but then reconsid-

ered, because there is already a book
called Overcoming Obstacles by Jill Siegal.
I did not want my book confused with
hers, plus I had a real problem with the
word overcome. You think of the word
"overcome" you think of mastering a
great challenge. That challenge is now
finished, it is done. Unfortunately for us,
those who are physically, or mentally
handicapped it is never over. We are
faced with new challenges everyday. For
every hurdle we climb over there are ten
more waiting right behind it. They change
in terms of their severity, but make no
mistake about it; we are always presented with new challenges. It's not fair, and
it's not fun, but such is the nature of the
beast.

    So I began reflecting over my life
and a memory came to surface. When I
was in fifth grade I recall being sent to
the school social worker. Now, I didn't
mind because this meant I got to miss
class (I wasn't a big fan of learning till
much later). So the social worker pointed
to a little nick-knack on her desk. It was
of a little boy fishing, and the caption
underneath said, "When life give you
lemons, make lemonade"
She turns to me and said "Brad do you

know what that means?"
I nodded my head that I did.
She asked me what I thought it meant.
I said, "It means to make the best out of
a bad situation."

   "That's correct", She said "and that
is what you need to do."
Even though I was only eleven at the
time, I thought gee, how profoundly stupid that is. To tell a child who had lost
the use of his left hand from a brain
tumor to just make the best out of
things. Look on the bright side; sure I
suppose you can do that if you're
deranged!

   I no longer have use of my legs
because of a car accident I was in, but on
the bright side both my arms still work.

   Oh joy, my wife left me today and is
taking me for everything I have, but I still
have my health.

   Somebody kidnapped my child, but
on the bright side I do have two more.

   My point is this, anyone who has
had a major tragedy happen to them is
bound to have strong emotions; feelings
of sadness, and anger among them. It is
wrong and insensitive to tell them "just
look on the bright side." It doesn't matter
whether you have Diabetes, Parkinson's,

Cancer, Multiple Sclerosis, Muscular
Dystrophy, AIDS, Brain Injury, Spinal Cord
Injury, Cerebral Palsy, etc., there is no
way to put a "positive spin" on these illnesses.

Then she says to me "Do you know
why your teacher sent you to see me?"

"Well, I guess sometimes I get sad" I
answered.

Then just when I thought she could-
n't possibly say anything more stupid
then what she had said prior she raises
the bar.

"Than don't," she said.

"Don't what?" I asked.

"Don't be sad. You're too young,
you have nothing to be sad about." She
stated as if this was self-apparent.

First of all what kind of dumb-ass
solution is that to a complex psychologi-
cal problem? They pay this woman to
dish out this crap. Did you have to earn a
degree to spit out such words of wisdom? If that's the case I think I can be a
social worker.

"What seems to be the problem?"

"I am anorexic"

"Don't be anorexic, eat something,
send in the next patient"

"What seems to be the problem?"

"I hear voices in my head."

"Don't listen to the voices anymore, turn on the radio instead. Next case."

It's one of the most moronic things I ever had said to me. The only other thing worse was when I heard a customer walk into Barnes and Noble and ask, "Excuse me do you sell books here?"

It is okay to be sad at times, especially when you have a chronic illness like those mentioned on the previous page. It is okay and it is normal. Anyone who tells you what your feeling is wrong, is a moron. It's only when your sad all the time that it becomes a problem. I will speak of depression more in a later chapter

When Life Gives You Lemons Make Lemonade. When you are faced with a minor inconvenience it's easy to spin it the other way. An example:
A neighbor's dog craps all over your back lawn, instead of getting upset you might say, "Hey maybe the fertilizer will help the grass grow better" For those of us who have a disability or illness the only "lemonade" would be a cure to our illness, to be "normal".

So finally, getting back to my title,

"When Life Gives You Lemons, Add
Tequila and Salt." When you walk into a
bar and you order tequila the bartender
will ask you "Do you want training wheels
with that?" The salt and the lemon are
the training wheels.

      People take them because with out
them the tequila is too strong. The salt
and lemon mask some of the taste of the
tequila. What I am suggesting is if you
find an activity or item that brings you
pleasure, that you can submerse yourself
in; it makes the illness easier to bear.
Find an outlet, be it sports, art, movies,
music, reading what ever. It won't make
the pain and suffering of your illness go
away but it will make your life more
enjoyable and you might make some
friends that have some similar interests
too. So that's how my book got its title, I
hope you enjoy the rest of my book.

Brad Goldstein

What we call
pleasure, and
rightly so is the
absence of all
pain.

F ORWARD

Now that I've explained what the
title of my book is about, let me tell you
why I decided to write it.

Six months after I had my stroke, I
seldom left my house alone. In fact, the
only time I left the house would be to go
to therapy or to accompany my parents,
relatives or close friends someplace.
However, my reasons for doing this are
probably not for the reasons you might

expect. It was not because I was afraid of falling or getting hurt. It was not because I couldn't drive, (because there was a bus stop right outside my development).

The reason was I was embarrassed. I didn't want to be seen, for reasons I will go into in another chapter. Nevertheless, it took approximately another two months before I gathered up the courage to leave my house alone. I got on the bus and I went to the local mall. Nothing exciting I went to a computer store and then I went to visit the store I worked at before my stroke. Now, understand I couldn't speak well enough to be understood at this point, and still can't always for that matter. Instead I used a machine to type into, and then I hit speak and the machine spoke the words I typed. It's very similar to the machine Steven Hawkins uses to speak (if you don't know who he is, don't worry I will get to it in a later chapter). Then I started to get hungry, so I stopped off at the food court to get some food. This is where my story truly begins.

I sat down to eat and noticed two middle aged women sitting at the table next table. (When I say middle aged I mean in their 40's. People often think

50's is middle aged, it is not unless you
plan to live to a hundred or older. Which
is a bit optimistic considering, currently
the average life span for woman in the
United States is 80.36. For men it is con-
siderably lower, by 6 years to be exact.)
What brought my attention to these two
ladies, was one of them had a loud high
pitched, shrill, irritating voice, that I'm
quite sure under the right circumstances
could shatter glass. You know the kind
that makes dogs whimper. Anyway, he
spoke with a New York accent but I didn't
have to listen to her voice to tell that she
was from New York. She waved her hands
and arms around when she spoke like she
was conducting an orchestra or trying to
signal a plane.

So her friend asked her how her
flight to Florida was, here was her
response (note the words in italics were
my sarcastic, smart-ass thoughts during
their conversation, if you can call it a
conversation. Usually when just one person bitches non-stop for 20 minutes you
call it a monologue, but I am getting
bogged down in semantics. Anyway
here's my short version of her relentless
complaints):

"Uy, yesterday was the most awful
day in my entire life." she said as she

threw back her head and rolled her eyes.

I wonder what percentages of people actually believe themselves when they say that. By the way when you haven't seen someone in a while and they start out by telling you "yesterday was the most awful day in my entire life", excuse yourself politely, like say "I have to use the restroom." Then climb into your car and drive away, if the person doing the bitching drove you call a cab. Trust me you will live much longer.

"So we arrived at the airport an hour early to do our bags and go through security and of course our plane was delayed an hour and a half. So we just had to wait at the terminal, I got up and complained to the flight-attendant at the counter 3 times."

Can you believe they made her and her family sit in an air-conditioned building, FOR OVER AN HOUR! Those Bastards.

"So the plane finally arrives..."

The plane was just an hour late; pull that pole out of your ass!! Opps, Sorry to interrupt.

"And I get stuck with the seat behind some four year old who is screaming and kicking my chair during the whole flight."

pg.XIII

She should actually consider herself
lucky; I always get stuck between the
drunk who farts during the entire flight
and over weight women with bad body
odor. You'll never find a scented candle
with those mixtures of aromas.

"Then to make matters worse..."

Oh my god, you mean it gets worse,
Opps I interrupted again.

"Jamie my youngest is whining his
ear is hurting him during the whole flight.
So we finally arrive at Ft. Lauderdale airport. The plane lost our luggage, can you
believe that?"

Can't you just hear the violins playing?

"We didn't get our luggage till this
morning."

Thank goodness, one more day
without her luggage and she would have
had a nervous brake-down.

The reason this lady, who I don't
know, got me so miffed, is quite simple. I
want to live this ladies life where the
biggest problems in my life are some
minor inconveniences on a flight to my
winter vacation. Because, after all that's
just what they were, minor, annoying,
insignificant inconveniences. Yes they're
stressful, yes they're frustrating, but we

all have to deal with them. However you live through it, and you put it behind you. Let me compare my worst day with hers.

I went to sleep Friday January 12, 2004 around midnight, but before I did I took some Tylenol and my allergy medication because I was beginning to get a headache. I woke up 4 o'clock in the morning, my headache was much worse now, my speech was beginning to sound garbled, and I was extremely dizzy. I didn't call 911 or wake my parents (a mistake I will regret for the rest of my life) because I had anxiety attacks in the past and the symptoms felt quite similar. I didn't want to have to make my parents pay for another visit to the hospital if all it was, was another anxiety attack.

I awoke at 8:00 in the morning and now my speech completely unintelligible, and I felt so weak. It wasn't like the kind of weakness you feel when you have a virus or the flu. My head ached and felt soar at the same time. It felt like someone had literally been bouncing my head off a brick wall all night. It felt too heavy to even lift up off the pillow. Yet, somehow at the same time, my head felt empty. Despite all my efforts to stay awake and go get help my eyes shut and

I began drifting back to sleep. I hoped
that all these symptoms were just a
result from being tired.

When I next woke up I believe it was
approximately 10:00. My body wanted
more sleep but something told me that if
I didn't get up and go for help, I might
not wake up again. It took all my effort
just to roll over, my body felt like a bag
of rocks. I managed to get one of my
legs off the bed and onto the floor. When
I tried to stand up my leg immediately
gave out against the weight of my body
and I came crashing down to my knees. I
crawled to my door and tried to lift my
right arm to turn the doorknob. Much to
my dismay my arm just remained at my
side, like the arm of corpse that had just
ceased to live. I used my other arm and
hand to turn the door knob which proved
to be quite difficult since that arm had
been mostly crippled from my brain
tumor when I was six. I managed to turn
the knob and saw my mother standing
behind the kitchen counter making herself
her morning breakfast. My body wobbled
from side to side as I desperately tried to
move forward towards her. With her help
I was able to get myself back to a standing position. She asked what was wrong,

pg.XVI

but I could only respond with incoherent
grunts and moans. I motioned for her to
give me a piece of paper, which she did. I
wrote in big scribble letters "can't move
arm, can't move leg, can't talk, please
help". She positioned me so I was leaning
against the counter and then ran to get
up my father. We called my cousin who is
a pharmacist and asked him what the
best hospital to bring me to was. Despite
being scared, I found that I was actually
laughing uncontrollably during all these
events, yet I felt no reason to be
amused. In the past I have started laughing when I felt nervous and I assumed
that was all this was. It would not be until
much later that it was explained to me
that uncontrollable, inappropriate laughter
can be a symptom of a stroke. All three
of us rushed down to Ft. Lauderdale to
go to the hospital. We filled out the information that they gave at the admissions
desk and waited for what seemed like
hours before I was taken into the emergency room. When that finally happened
various doctors saw me and tests were
done. The doctors reviewed my tests and
finally gave my family and I their progno-
sis. At only 25 years, I, Brad Goldstein
had suffered a stroke.

Yet, despite this all January 13, 2004 was not the worst day of my life. Because right before my parents, had me admitted to intensive care, kissed me goodbye and then left the hospital. My mother asked me if I was scared. I could not speak so I used a board they had given me with all the letters of the alphabet on it. I spelled out "no". My mom shocked said "why not?" I said I am only 25 years old I could not have had a stroke, this all must just be a bad dream. I was in such a state of denial; I believed this without a doubt in my mind. I was certain that any minute I would wake up and I would be at home in my bed. My body would be as it always was, and all of this would be a fading memory. The day after was the worst day of my life, because on that day it became real.

So that was my worst day, do you think that lady at the mall would like to trade? I don't think she would, after all if she can't handle a 1 hour plane delay I doubt she can handle a stroke.

You listen to what people complain about and the most common thing is the weather. It's to hot, it's to cold, it's to damp, it's to dry. The second most com-

plaint is traffic. It all doesn't mean
SHIT. Because at the end of the day
you put all that crap behind you and you
awake the next morning hoping for a better day. I don't get to sweep it all under
the rug and start a new.I know tomorow
morning when I wake up I still won't be
able to speak properly.

Healthy people can be as sympathetic as they want to be, but they can
never fully understand the inner pain I
suffer day after day, night after night.
That was when it hit me. Sitting at the
table at the mall. They have no idea.
Healthy people have no idea. There lies
the inspiration behind the book. So to the
lady who was bitching at the mall over
miniscule things, I say thank you.

Even though I can describe in great
vivid detail. My pain and suffering over
what only amounts to 20 years. I know I
can't even begin to show you the pain I
feel. The large empty void that I feel
deep within side me, that I pray will
someday be filled. The aching longing for
a cure, or hope that one day my brain will
repair itself. The self misdirected hatred
that sometimes seers deep within side
me. I keep replaying the night of my

pg.XIX

stroke over and over again. I drown in
guilt from wondering, had I not gone back
to sleep, had I called for help would I be
different. Also guilt from complaining
before my stroke, over insignificant
things like the lady at the mall. The
Jealousy that I have to constantly sup-
press and hide, over all the people that
live happy, healthy lives unscathed. I can
describe these things but in the end I
know they're just words.

However if I can even give you a
glimpse into the pain and suffering of one
who was unfortunate enough, to not just
be struck once but twice by tragedy in a
short lifetime. Then I have accomplished
my goal. I hope you can learn something
to from the mistakes I have made too.
Enjoy the rest of my book.

ISBN: 978-0-6151-6048-1

When Life Gives You Lemons Add Tequila And Salt

By Brad Goldstein

Title Page

I had to train myself to focus my attention. I became very visual and learned how to create mental images in order to comprehend what I read.

Tom Cruise

Elementary School
&
Learning Disablities

I have a very extensive long-term memory. (I have a horrible short-term memory, which I will go into later in this chapter.) I can remember vividly the crib I slept in as a baby. However I cannot recall most of the year I spent in the hospital. I cannot remember at all the time I spent in the hospital in New York when I was 6 years old. That was where I had the laser surgery by Doctor Epsteine. I remember bits and pieces of the time I spent in Children's Memorial Hospital in Chicago where I got the radiation and spent my recovery.

I missed months of school in the time I was hospitalized. Luckily I was only in Kindergarten; otherwise I probably would have had to repeat the year. I do recall the day I came back from the hospital. First of all my head had been completely shaved for the surgery and not very little of my hair had grown back yet.

I remember walking into the classroom and the students were all sitting down together like kids do at story time. I felt the children had obviously been prepped for my coming since no-one looked shocked to see me in fact they had hardly any reaction at all when I walked in the door, except maybe some smiles. I sat in the front of the class and explained where I had been all that time. I told stories about being in the hospital.

Then I was on to first grade. For information on my experience in first grade see my chapter regarding <u>Prejudice and Apathy</u>. Since nothing else of any importance happened I will move on to 2nd grade.

The Reader might be interested in

knowing that these chapters were not
written in sequential order. This was not
intentional, but is not unusual for me
because I often don't work from the
beginning of project to the end. Often I'll
have an idea how 5th page in a website
should look before the 1st one. To most
people this would seem disorganized but
it works for me because organization is
one of my learning disabilities.

    It was in 2nd grade that I was put
into special education for part of the day.
Some people thought I had learning diffi-
culties as a result from all the radiation I
had undergone while in the hospital, however that was never certain. Mostly I
needed help with spelling and my hand-
writing. Later on this would not be as big
a problem I simply used the computer to
type and spell check all my work, but in
elementary school all our work was hand
written. I don't believe they really tested
me to see where my problem areas were;
I just brought in whatever work I needed
help in to Special Ed.

    There was a definitely a negative
stigma associated with being in special
education in my elementary school. They
were known as the "dumb" kids, the

"retards". It was well known that several
of the Special Education kids had behav-
ioral problems as well. They even had a
separate table where they all ate with the
teacher. They were the outcast in early
elementary school. Since I only had to be
with them for part of the day and I didn't
want any of the negative social impacts I
acted very secretly. When I left my main
classroom I never told anyone where I
was really going (except my teacher of
course). When I was in the Special Ed
room I spoke to all the Special Ed students. However when I was with my regular classmates if one of the Special Ed
students said hello to me in the hall, I
pretended I didn't know who they were. It
was really quite terrible the way I acted
towards them, but realize Special Ed students or DSL students as they were
called in my school were not socially
accepted. By 4th grade students in my
regular class knew where I was going but
by then they didn't care.

By 5th grade they mainstreamed
the Special Ed students with the regular
students. So we only went to Special Ed
for one period (there were 9 periods in
the day). By 5th grade nobody really

pg.4

cared if you were in a Special Ed class
anyway. The great thing about being in
Special Ed for part of the day was if one
of your teachers were not being accom-
modating to a student with special needs,
they would help resolve the issues. The
hardest thing for me was anything that
involved a lot of memorization. We had a
test on Geography where we had to know
where each of the 50 states were on a
blank map. I still till this day can't do it.
(However my freshman year of high
school we were required to memorize 20
lines of Romeo and Juliet. For each line
above and beyond that would bring up a
test score 1 point (which I desperately
needed) so consequently I memorized
120 lines. It took me a month to learn)

This is how it remained for me all
the way until freshman year of High
School. By freshman year of High School I
wanted out of Special Ed. It had nothing
to do with any social stigmas I was just
bored. I didn't need the help anymore so I
slept through most of my Resource class
(Actually I slept in a lot of classes in
High School). So I dropped out of special
Ed but I still needed accommodations. So
I was administered an IQ test by a Social
Worker to see what accommodations

pg.5

were needed. These were my accommodations:

More time on tests if needed.
Take tests in distraction free environment
if needed.
More time to get to class if needed
Limit the amount of memorization
required where applicable
Provide a word-bank on fill in the blank
questions

There were always students who
complained "How come he gets a different test than us", "How come he doesn't
get a detention when he's late"," How
come he gets more time on his paper".
One time a parent called in to complain it
wasn't fair I was getting special treatment.

My teacher responded by saying "I
am not at liberty to discuss Mr.
Goldstein's situation with you, but just be
glad your son or daughter doesn't have
all the problems he has."

There were also students who
abused their accommodations, and made
it more difficult for the rest of us. One
time a student went up to the instructor
and asked for more time on his term
paper, which was one of his accommodations. So I asked him out of curiosity

"Are you almost done with yours?"

"You kidding I haven't even started it yet"

See he didn't need more time; he just needed to stop being a slacking, lazy, procrastinator.

Occasionally I had instructors who were not willing to accommodate me and I didn't always handle that well, as you will see in a later chapter.

Now it seems like learning disabilities are becoming more common-place. Tons of kids are labeled ADD (Attention Deficit Disorder), AD/HD (Attention-deficit/hyperactivity disorder), and Dyslexia. Nevertheless people seem reluctant to talk about it. When I hear parents talk about their children having a learning disability they most often whisper. Your son or daughter has a learning disability they didn't rob a bank! It is nothing to be ashamed or embarrassed about. The fact that you're whispering sends a message to your child that there is something to be embarrassed about. If the reason you are whispering is because your child doesn't like you discussing it with other people, then shame on you for not respecting your child's wishes. Though I would encourage your child to be upfront with it

rather than make excuses. The more
commonplace you allow learning disabilities to become the less it will be an issue.

Now it seems like for every child
who brings home an "F" on a test, there
is a parent who is ready to run to get
there child tested for a learning disability.
However before you get in your car and
subject your child to the most boring,
and partially condescending test they will
ever take in their life (I say partially condescending because the way the IQ test
works is, it starts off ridiculously easy
and then gets progressively harder. I had
such an arrogant ego back when I took
the test I thought the social worker was
patronizing me. My greatest pet peeve is
being patronized and I don't take it well),
consider getting them a tutor or letting
them stay after school to work on the
subject with their children. I say this
because perhaps your child doesn't have
a learning disability but is just poor in
that one subject. We all can't be good at
everything. People who have a left dominant brain are usually better at math and
science. People with a left dominant brain
tend to be more logical and sequential.
People who have a right dominant brain
are usually better at English and Social

Studies. Right brain people tend to look
at the big picture and are more intuitive.
Without going into a deep explanation
lets say that people who use one dominant side of their brain more than the
other process information differently. In
High School I was terrible at math and
science. I couldn't remember all of the
equations, symbols for different elements
and such. However I was great in geometry, because geometry is all visual which
right-brained people are more visual.

I was always good at thinking
"Outside the box", a term that has
become so over used recently that it has
become cliché. A fact I find somewhat
amusing since very few people actually
know what the term means. My junior
year of high school my Chemistry teacher
gave us a great project. She split us all
up into groups and then assigned each
group an item. My group she told us "I
want you to tell me how a cardboard box
is made. You can use books, magazines,
inter-net, interviewing a company I don't
care, but the information will not be in
your Chemistry book. Then you must
teach the class how boxes are made.
Wow, you mean I actually get to think for
myself, how innovative. Because if you

pg.9

think about 90 percent of the stuff you
learn in school is just regurgitating the
information from the class book. How
often in life when you have a problem, is
the answer sitting right in front of you?
Not very often. If you ask me, the educa-
tional system should be teaching children
how to find the answers for themselves,
rather than just always giving it to them.

There are six different ways in which
we effectively learn information: hearing,
seeing, reading, writing, illustration and
first hand experience. When I was in
school information was primarily taught
through our classroom book (reading)
and Secondary through class lecture
(hearing). I am an audio-visual learner so I
learned best from filmstrips and videos,
and lectures that were accompanied by
an over-head presentation. If I was given
a passage to read, I read I immediately
forgot it. The point is the most effective
way to teach is by applying all six methods of learning. The technology that is
available today is far greater than it was
when I was in school. Teachers should use
technology to appeal to all 6 of the
methods in which we learn. Instructors
who insist on teaching with the traditional
method of just book and lecture are

obsolete and will hopefully become
extinct like the dinosaurs. Teachers who
are innovative and make learning interesting and fun have the greatest chance of
reaching all their students.

"An ounce of prevention is worth a pound of cure."
-Henry de Bracton ,De Legibus , 1240

Stroke and Stroke Prevention

I sincerely hope that if you gain nothing else from this book, that you receive some knowledge from this chapter. If you read my Forward I described what having a stroke was like for me. The thing that makes strokes so hard to self diagnose is the symptoms vary for everyone. Furthermore, the symptoms for stroke are similar to many other illnesses. The following are symptoms of stroke:

Unexplained	Sudden numbness or weakness of the face, arm, or leg particularly on one side of the body
Confusion	
Trouble	talking or understanding
Sudden	vision problems
Sudden	walking problems
Dizziness	loss of balance or coordination
Unexplained	and sudden headache
Sudden	nausea, vomiting, and fever
Loss	of or decreased consciousness

If you have more than one of these symptoms I urge you to call 911 immediately. Should you decide not to call emergency medical service, do this one thing; take an Aspirin or Aspirin equivalent like Bayer. Do not take Tylenol or a Tylenol equivalent, it won't help your situation. Aspirin is a blood thinner. Strokes are caused when oxygen cannot reach the cells in your brain. This is most commonly caused when there is a blood clot in an artery that goes to the brain or occasionally by low blood pressure. Another, less common cause of stroke is from hemorrhaging or bleeding inside the brain. Hemorrhaging is usually caused by high blood pressure.

People over the age of 50, people
with high cholesterol, high or low blood
pressure, diabetics, people who received
high dosages of radiation, heavy drinkers,
people who smoke, and people who use
illegal drugs are all at higher risk for having a stroke. If you fit into one or more of
these categories you may want to ask
your physician about starting aspirin therapy. I would not advise going on aspirin
therapy without speaking to your doctor
because there are risk factors. Side
affects include bruising easily and your
blood does not clot as quickly. If you are
allergic to aspirin there are other blood
thinners you can take. Again, ask your
doctor before you take any blood thinner.

The best cure for worry, depression, melancholy, brooding, is to go deliberately forth and try to lift with one's sympathy the gloom of somebody else.

Arnold Bennet

Accident Prone/Sympathy Whore
Dont try this at home"

Bumps, cuts, sprains, bruises, and breaks, all children get them, but when you are physically disabled you get them more. By age 13 I had been to the hospital for a broken shoulder bone, double hernia surgery, 7 stitches in my forehead, inflammation of the hip, and asthma (which is unrelated to my physical disability but I had to go to the emergency room several times as a child for it.). This is not even counting all the hospital visits I had to go to check on my growth hormone and shunt. I've heard these things referred to as the battle scars of growing up. If that is true I had more than my share of battles.

However, I can't blame all these injuries on my disability alone. I was a very adventurous child. An adventurous spirit and a disabled left hand and partially disabled leg make for a dangerous combination. While I was recollecting over some of the dangerous stunts I pulled as a child, the words "What The Hell Was I Thinking" kept repeating itself. Here are some of the stunts:

My sister who is four and a half years older than me once suggested that we go riding down a steep sidewalk on her bike together, with her sitting in the bike seat and myself sitting on the handlebars. Miraculously we made it the bottom of the slope without injury.

So this led me to a brilliant idea. I bet I could go down the slope by myself sitting on my bike's handlebars. My theory was that I could steer my bike with my ass. Well... you can guess this experiment didn't turn out too well. My bike rolled about 4 inches and then flipped over. I as a result went face first into the sidewalk and sprained my wrist and scraped my knees and elbows. I never took physics but I'll take a crack at explaining why this didn't work. With my sister sitting in the bike seat there was an equal proportion of weight distributed on both ends of the bike. However when I attempted to do it alone all the weight was on the front of the bike causing the bike to topple over. Case in point, DON'T TRY THIS AT HOME KIDS!!!

There was another place near my house where I used to ride my bike. This had a steep hill as well. To add to the excitement this slope had a low branch coming off of a nearby tree. So once your bike began to pick up speed at the top of the hill you had to duck or else you would get smacked in the face with the branch. When I was little they showed reruns of the cartoon George Of The Jungle (Watch Out For That Tree!!). George was a Tarzan like character who went swinging from trees. So naturally I began to think "you know if I grabbed that branch at just the right moment, I bet I could swing from the tree branch and then jump down to the sidewalk. What the hell made me think I was capable of such a feat? I have no idea, but it seemed like a good idea at the time.

It took me about 10 times before I was able to time it so I could grab the

pg.17

branch on my way down the hill. The
results did not work out as planned. If
you ever studied Newton's laws of motion
you know, "a body in motion stays in
motion, unless an equal or greater force
is exerted against it." Therefore when I
grabbed the branch my body stopped
moving, but the bike did not. This caused
the pedals of my bike to wrap themselves
around my feet. I was lifted off the seat
of my bike and tossed into the air along
with my bike. I landed flat on my back
and looked up just in time to see the
wheel of my bike come crashing down on
my genitals. I was walking funny the next
few days as a result. Obviously I missed
the point of George Of The Jungle
because George was always slamming
into trees and getting hurt. Again, DON'T
TRY THIS AT HOME KIDS!!!

Those are just two examples of stupid stunts I attempted that caused me
injury. I'd list them all but they would
take up a book in themselves. I learned
several important lessons from these
events. Like don't swat a bee's nest with
a fly swatter, and don't tease the neigh-
borhood pit-bull.

As far back as I can remember I

have craved attention. Usually when children are starved for attention it is for
either one of the two reasons. Either the
child is not getting any attention at home
and thus goes looking for it in other
places or the child gets to much attention at home and thus expects it every
where else as well. However, before you
go getting all analytical let me dispel the
notion that neither of these scenarios
was the case. My parents paid ample
amounts of attention to both my sister
and I, however they were careful not to
spoil us by giving us too much attention.

If you remembered in the last chapter I discussed how nice the children were
when I came back to the hospital. That
soon quickly changed. There was a
tremendous emphasis on sports at my
school. I remember parents literally forc-
ing their kids to join little league despite
their child's objection. Sports were the
primary way in which boys in my community met, socialized and made friends. At
recess when we were picking teams I was
always the last to be picked. As you can
imagine this doesn't do a hell of a lot for
a child's self esteem growing up. I could

not compete in most sports and further
more had no interest in it either.
Consequently I drifted apart from my
friends for whom sports was a major part
of their life. I became somewhat with-
drawn from the other children at school.

I had problems developing relation-
ships with people. That started way back
in elementary school and still continues
till this day. My people skills are negligible
at best.

The only thing good about being
injured was the over abundance of sympathy I received from my classmates at
school. So naturally I milked it for all it
was worth. I became a world-class sympathy whore. A classmate, who would
inquire about what was wrong with my
hand, would receive the entire sob story
about my tumor and my time spent at
the hospital. The problem with sympathy
is it never lasts. Eventually people get
tired of hearing about your problems and
don't want to hear about it any longer.

I don't fault the children at school
for being sympathetic. People should be
sympathetic to those that are disabled. I
put the blame squarely on me for milking

it the way I did. However, I did not take
kindly to pity. There is a big difference
between sympathy and pity. Here's my
illustration:

A. "Let me see if Brad needs help
cutting that piece of paper." =
Sympathetic

B. "Do you see the way his hand is
hanging, yuck, I would kill myself if that
happened to me" = Pity

Pity is not helpful. I recall on one occasion
I was playing kickball and the pitcher,
pitched the ball normally to the child that
was up to bat. Then when I was up the
pitcher pitched the ball really slow to me.
So I picked the ball up.

"What the hell, pitch the ball normally!" I yelled.

"But you will miss if I pitch it fast,"
He yelled back.

"Probably, but at least I will have
earned it."

The way I looked at it, it's only a game. If
I miss the ball, I miss. However if I get on
base at least I know that it was because
of my efforts.

Ultimately I would find different and
better ways of receiving attention at

school. I became the class-clown, which
had mixed results and sometimes got me
into trouble when I took it to far. I will
go into that further later on. For now let
me conclude by saying this, If you are
using your injury as the primary source
for receiving attention from your peers. I
suggest you find another way to get people to take interest in you. The reason is
sympathy is waning. My suggestion, find
something your good at and make friends
that have a common interest.

You may be wondering why I choose
to put the two topics together in one
chapter like this, (Sympathy Whore and
Accident Prone), for this was not my
original intention. As I was thinking about
the two chapters a thought occurred to
me. On a subconscious level was there a
connection to the attention I was receiving and my injuries I sustained as a child.
In other words, on some level was I taking
these risks to purposefully injure myself
to gain attention. It is a question I can't
answer because these events took place
over 15 years ago and furthermore if
they were subconscious I wouldn't know
about them anyway. However, it is just

pg.22

another reason not to be a sympathy
whore.

Doctors are men who prescribe medicines of which they know little, to cure diseases of which they know less in human beings of whom they know nothing.

Voltaire (1694 - 1778)

D OCTORS ARE NOT GODS

(Although they make more money then he does)

Most people have a very narrow definition of a doctor. Simply put, a doctor is someone you go to when you feel ill to make you feel better. Their role is very clear; they diagnosis your condition and prescribe medication to fix that condition. You say "doctor" and everyone pictures a

man or woman in a white lab coat with a
stethoscope around his or her neck. For
those of us who are disabled or suffer
from chronic illness, a doctor is so much
more. If you question the validity of my
opinions on this subject, which I suspect
you might, consider this: I have spent
more hours with doctors and in hospitals
than I have spent in movie theatres during my lifetime. I've gone to the movies a
lot in 26 years but I have spent months
at hospitals when I was an inpatient. I
know a thing or two about doctors.

There are people who go into the
medical profession with the noblest of
intentions. If you ask a first year med
student, "Why do you want to be a doctor?" they might answer back, "I want to
help people." When you ask other first
year med students the same question,
you will get an entirely different answer. "
I want to be a doctor because they make
a lot of money" or "I want to be a doctor
because my father was a doctor and my
grandfather was a doctor."

If you ever end up in the emergency
room, I'll bet you would want the doctor
who gave response number one working
on you; those are the doctors that are
going to go above and beyond the call of

duty for their patients. A doctor is supposed to give you hope. A doctor is supposed to fight your illness with all his will as if the illness was his own.

In other forms of work, occasionally you have an employee who for whatever reason doesn't give work his best effort on a particular day. In other forms of work you may even occasionally make a mistake. Hopefully if you a have a boss or supervisor he or she will catch your mistake and you can go back and fix it. In the medical profession, however there is no room for mistakes. If a doctor makes a mistake a patient can die. It is for this reason we hold doctors to a higher standard than we do other professions. Nonetheless mistakes are made in the medical profession every day.

Several years ago there was a man whose leg became infected. In order to stop the infection from spreading his doctor decided that he needed to amputate the leg. The doctor marked on the chart which leg needed to be amputated, as well as marked the leg itself with a big "X" in black marker. The patient was then given an anesthetic and then he was moved to surgery where his leg was surgically amputated. When the patient

awoke in post op he lifted the bed sheets
to see how his body looked with the
missing leg. He was horrified to find the
leg marked with the "X" was still
attached to his body. The surgeon amputated the wrong leg. The infected leg
would have to still be amputated, which
meant the man would no longer have
legs. With one leg the man could have
received a prosthetic leg and still been
able to walk. Instead he had no legs and
would have to use a wheelchair for mobility for the rest of his life. The man sued
the hospital and the surgeon for millions,
but all the money in the world would not
give this man back his leg.

The point of this tragic and true
story is that doctors do indeed make mistakes. When I was 6 years old my mom
took me to our pediatrician because my
left hand was shaking involuntarily.

My pediatrician said, "It's probably
just nerves, it will go away on its own."
(Now logically at 6 years of age what reason could I possibly have to be nervous?
What did he think I could possibly be
nervous about?)

A few months later my mother
took me back to the doctor to report
that my hand was shaking worse.

pg.27

Again my pediatrician said, "It's probably just nerves it will go away on its own."

A few months later my mom took me back to my pediatrician again to report my hand was still getting worse. Finally the doctor ordered some CAT scans of my brain. The reason my hand was shaking was that I had a brain tumor pressing against my brain stem. My parents asked the neurologist if waiting all those months could have possibly made me worse. My neurologist said probably not, but I will never know for sure. Everyone always asks me why we didn't sue my pediatrician; we certainly had a strong case. What they don't realize is that I was hospitalized for a few months in New York, then in Chicago. It took me months to recover. My parents could have concentrated on suing my pediatrician or concentrated on getting me better. I think they made the right choice.

What the doctor should have done was, The first time I walked in, say "I don't think it is anything, but lets check you out with a CAT scan to make sure."

A tragic mistake was made to my friend's mother. One day she was showering and felt a lump on her breast. She

pg.28

went to the doctor to get a mammogram, but nothing showed up on the
mammogram. The doctor said, "Why
don't you come back in three months and
we will see if anything shows up. Her family begged her to get a second opinion.
They said 3 months is too long to wait if
you think it might be cancer. Despite her
family's objections, she waited 3 months
and returned to her doctor. The doctor
could only say "I'm sorry, the results indi-
cate you have breast cancer." By then it
was too late, the cancer having already
spread through her lymph nodes. She
tried chemo therapy and different medicines but nothing worked.

The second mistake that was done
to me also occurred to me when I was 6.
The doctor told my parents "given the
amount of radiation your son received it
would not be unusual if he were to have a
stroke in the future". So here's the mil-
lion-dollar question, knowing this why did-
n't they start me on preventative aspirin
therapy? Aspirin is a blood thinner and
would have most likely prevented me
from having a stroke. A girl who was in
the hospital at the same time I was, had
3 strokes and her doctors still didn't
place her on aspirin therapy.

pg.29

Doctors do make mistakes, what are the measures you can take to insure you these mistakes don't happen to you?

1. When your regular physician refers you
to a specialist ask him what he thinks the
illness could be? Then go to the library or
Internet and familiarize yourself with that illness.

2. Ask a lot of questions: Once you have been referred to a specialist, create a
list of questions for the doctor.

3. If the doctor says you have cancer or any other major illness, find out who is consid ered the best doctor in the state, if
you have the financial means to travel find the best in the country or even the world .

4. If you think a doctor might be mistaken
get a second opinion.

In my grandfather's generation, the men and women revered their doctors as gods. You never questioned the doctor. You followed the doctor's instructions without hesitation and without discussion. After all, the doctor has a medical degree and a level of understanding of your illness that is far superior to yours. Today

with increasing availability and access to
the internet as wel as library resources
patients can and do research on there
own illnesses. Patients are more educated
and do not hesitate to discuss treatment
options with their doctor.

Some doctors don't like when you
ask them questions. When my dad
accompanied my grandfather to the doctor he brought with him a list of questions for the doctor about my grandfa-
thers treatment.

He said to the doctor, "I have a few
questions to ask you if you don't mind."

The doctor turned to him and said,
"I don't have to answer any of your questions."

Legally he is right, but what harm
could it possibly do to answer the questions my father had. It's not a stranger
asking the question; it is my grandfather's son. Here's the way I look at it;
you're paying the doctor, and he works
for you. If the doctor says he is too busy
or acts like you are bothering him, find
another doctor. If you're in an HMO and
you can't switch doctor's, find out what
hospital he is affiliated with and report
him. Remember everyone has to report to
someone, there has to be a medical

board you can complain to. The point is
to make some noise.

Two years ago I had a concussion. I
was diagnosed and medicated to stop the
pain but the medication made me real
drowsy. I called my doctor to ask him a
question about the medication:

"Hi I'd like to speak to the doctor," I
said.

"I'm sorry but the doctor doesn't
come to the phone," said his secretary.

"Oh, well I can call back during his
lunch hour if you would like," I said.

"No I mean he doesn't answer questions over the phone. You will have to
make an appointment for an office visit if
you have questions," she stated.

"But I was just there yesterday," I
shouted.

"Well I am sorry, that is his policy,"
she answered.

"So I have to pay 160 dollars for an
office visit, for a question concerning the
medication he prescribed me yesterday?"
I asked.

"Yes, that is what I am telling you sir,"

"Okay well be sure to tell the doctor
his policy sucks, and if I get sick or die
from taking the medication wrong; it's his
ass that's going to get sued by my fami-

pg.32

ly," I shouted and hung up the phone.

Obviously the doctor can have that policy because people let him get away with it. He figures this way he can squeeze another 160 dollars out of patients. I don't know what it is about the white lab coat that makes people completely submissive. In no other industry that I know of will people accept such sub par service. There must be some intimidation factor that I am missing. In fact Stanley Milgram did a study on people and authority figures in 1974.

"In most versions of this experiment two individuals would arrive at a testing center simultaneously. Here they would meet an instructor who appeared to be conducting the experiment. This instructor superficially appeared as an authority figure by displaying the necessary credentials as a professor such as a white lab coat and clipboard. The two "subjects" were then taken to a room where one was strapped in a chair to prevent movement and an electrode was placed on their arm. Next, the other individual who was called the "teacher" was taken to an adjoining room where he/she was instructed to read a list of two word pairs. He/She would then ask the "learn-

er" to read them back. If the "learner"
got the answer correct, they would then
move on to the next set of words in the
series. However, if the answer was wrong
the "teacher" was informed by the
instructor that they were required to
administer shock to the "learner". These
shocks first started at 15 volts and
increased to 450 volts for each incorrect
response. This occurred in 15-volt incre-
ments. The "teacher" was never coersed
into doing so they were simply told by
the instructor that the experiment
required them to continue. This in fact is
what made this study so intriguing; the
"teacher" could have discontinued the
experiment at any time but the majority
continued to shock. The "teacher" was
fully under the assumption that he/she
was administering discipline to the "learner" however; they were never really doing
so. The "learner" was actually a confeder-
ate, a student or actor, who were never
actually harmed. This version was
Miligram's experiment was the most
basic. There were numerous variations in
the arrangement between the "learner"
and the "teacher" which entailed the
proximity of the victim to the disciplinari-
an and others where there were contra-

pg.34

dictions between numerous instructors as
to whether the experiment should go on
just to name a few." http://members.tri-
pod.com/mikeg531/MikeG531.htm

There is something about the doctor
patient relationship that turns ordinary
intelligent people into mindless zombies.
It amazes me why people would pay for
inadequate service and abuse. Trust me
there are plenty of good doctors it yours
is not one of them I urge you to switch.
I have one last story to tell. Four years
ago I had, what the doctors now believe
was another stroke. It didn't show up on
the catscan, and was finally diagnosed as
a result of migraines. The problem was
with my eyes. One of my eyes was moving independantly of the other. I had
gone to two eye doctors, an ear nose
and throat doctor, and a neurologist. No
one was able to figure out what was
wrong with my eyes. Finally my mother
asked who the best eye doctor in the city
of Chicago was. It was months before I
could get an appointment. The doctor ran
a series of eye tests on me. After the
tests were done he asked to speak to my
mother alone.

"Do you know what's wrong? She
asked.

"Yes I do," he replied "There's absolutely nothing physically wrong with him, your son's either nuts or faking it."

Honestly, if I could purposely make one of my eyes move without the other, I'd go on Letterman because that would be quite a trick. I took a whole lot of restraint not to strike the doctor. So once again, I'd like to point out the doctor made a mistake. Not only did he make a mistake but he was rude and insulting as well. Nobody has to take that kind of crap from a doctor. Don't put up with a doctor who is treating you badly.

Prejudice is opinion

without judgement.
Voltaire
French author, humanist, rationalist,
& satirist (1694 - 1778)

Prejudice
and Apathy

Whether you are Black, White,
Hispanic, Asian, Indian, Native American,
Arab, Muslim, Gay, Straight, Bisexual,
Republican, Democrat, Catholic,
Protestant, Lutheran, Episcopalian,
Quaker, Amish, Atheist, Agnostic, Jewish,
Buddhist, Hindu, or any other nationality,
Fat, Skinny, Tall, Short, Male or Female
there is a whole group of people some-
where in the world that hate you. (I apol-
ogize if I left your group out.) Our par-

pg.37

ents, our brothers and sisters, aunts and
uncles, our grandparents, our friends, and
our religious organizations all pass on
prejudice. Prejudices can also be caused
by traumatic, life changing events. All
prejudices come from one of these 3
reasons:
They look differently,
They act differently,
They think differently,
Then I do. Every war ever fought was
fought for one of these three reasons. I
don't like prejudice but I understand
where it comes from and I understand it
is not going away. Nevertheless, the one
prejudice I can't understand is prejudice
towards the physically and mentally handicapped.

     It doesn't make sense to me,
because anyone can suddenly become
disabled. No one is exempt from being
disabled. It doesn't matter what ethnicity
you are, where you're from, or what you
look like; a life changing experience can
render you permanently disabled for the
rest of your life. Even if you don't
believe in karma, there is always the pos-
sibility that you will develop an illness
during your lifetime. Very few people die
of old age alone. You're statistically more

pg.38

likely to die of cancer or one of many
other life threatening diseases that are
out there. So why anyone would inten-
tionally cause grief to a physically or
mentally disabled person is beyond me. I
don't think mistreating disabled people is
a learned behavior like other prejudices.
No educated adult with half a brain would
teach a child to be mean to a disabled
person.

For me, growing up with a physical
disability was like growing up with a bull's
eye painted on my stomach. Having a disability made you the target of every dis-
contented, socially dysfunctional child in
my school. When we were picking teams
for sports I was always the last one
picked. I recall one occasion were the two
captains got into an argument over who
had to take me for their team. (It always
makes you feel good to be wanted.)

I remember discussing with my
school social worker the reason other
children picked on me all the time. She
said they were scared of me because on
a subconscious level they were afraid
that something similar could happen to
them. I do understand how fear has a
way of manifesting itself into hate, but I
think that her explanation is far too com-

plicated for an elementary school child. I
think the simple reason why I got picked
on was because I was easy prey. When
animals are hunting a heard they always
go after the slowest, weakest animal in
the herd first. If one animal in the herd is
injured, he or she becomes the sacrificial
lamb for the group. If you think about it,
it makes perfect sense. If you are going
to bully someone, are you going to go
after the tallest, strongest kid who is
always surrounded by his friends in the
class or the tiny, weak kid that sits all
alone?

It took me a while even as an adult
to put all that stuff behind me. Yet even
as an adult I am still faced with people
who view me as an object of ridicule.
People laugh; people whisper little com-
ments to each other when I walk by,
sometimes they look at me with disgust,
and sometimes they look at me with pity.
They see me as less of a person, a broken vessel, incomplete. I guess if an ignorant person views a perfectly healthy person as whole you could make the argument that a disabled person is less than
whole.

I have come to realize ignorance is
not the only reason people avoid disabled

people. I remember on one occasion I
went to fast food restaurant and the
gentleman behind the register kept giving
me a dirty look and rolling his eyes while I
was typing out a message on my
machine. Come on you're holding up the
line and I don't have the patience to deal
with it. Hey, you think it's annoying, you
only have to deal with it for 5 minutes
while I order a sandwich, I have to deal
with it every day.

Admittedly I myself am not a
patient person which is one of the reasons not being able to talk well is such a
big deal to me. Here's my theory: some
people are so set in their ways and so
rigid that they put themselves in a bubble. They're happy and content as long as
everything remains status quo. Should
you do anything remotely different to
them, however it bursts their bubble.

A few months ago I was at a restaurant and my mom ordered a coke for me.
She said to the waitress "no ice please in
that, my son has a swallowing problem
and it will make him choke". It was less
then a second but the women shook her
head and rolled her eyes. You might have
thought my mother was asking her for a
kidney instead of no ice in a drink. I could

read what that look meant, all the other customers don't make special requests about their drinks. They drink it like I give it to them. We busted her comfort bubble.

I have a service dog; it helps me pick up objects I drop, and get up off the ground. I am allowed to bring her anywhere, same as a seeing eye dog or dog for the hearing impaired. Occasionally I will enter an establishment and hear a group of cranky, irritating senior citizens talking to each other saying, " Is that a dog?", "Is he bringing a dog into the restaurant?", "Why is he bringing a dog into the restaurant?", "I never heard of anyone bringing a dog into a restaurant.", "Who brings a dog into a restaurant?", "I don't understand." Here's a thought, why not try minding your own damn business? I burst their comfort bubble.

The following story really irritates me. 3 months after I suffered a stroke I was finally released. I was 24 at the time. I was out of the hospital no longer than 2 or 3 weeks. My parents took me shopping with them to buy shoes. At the time I still did not have great balance, so my parents took me in my wheel chair. After we purchased shoes my parents decided to

stop by the men's department to look at
shirts for my dad. My parents wheeled me
into an empty isle and put down my
security break so my wheelchair wouldn't
move. Along comes an elderly couple,
who must have assumed I was deaf
because they made no attempt to lower
their voice.

Elderly Woman: "Would you just look
at that? I can't stand that."

Elderly Man: "What, what are you
talking about?"

Elderly Woman: "Can't you see? He's
blocking the whole isle with his chair."

Elderly Man: "So what do you care?
He's in the men's department."

Elderly Woman: "So what if I wanted
to buy you a shirt, I can't get down that
isle because his damn wheelchair is blocking the whole damn isle. These disabled
people think they own the whole world;
the whole world revolves around them.
Like the whole world has to stop turning
just because a disabled person needs a
place to park his chair."

Elderly Man: "So if you want to get
down there you go down the next isle or
the previous one."

Elderly Woman: "Why should I have
to inconvenience myself by going down a

pg.43

different isle? He shouldn't be allowed to block an isle with his chair. It's bad enough they get all the best parking spots, now they get to take up entire isles."

At this point I figured it would take me too long to type something nasty into my speaking machine. So I simply gave her the one finger salute. Yes, the universal sign for "what you're saying displeases me". Her husband laughed and she gasped. Yes indeed, I burst her comfort bubble.

I have spent more than a few minutes thinking about a possible scenario that might have happened in this woman's life to have caused this woman to be such a high strung, inconsiderate, self-centered bitch. So far, the only one I can come up with is maybe at some point a small, furry, rabid rodent crawled up her ass and now it's babies are trying to burrow their way out. A situation that severe would make this woman's actions not to be deemed totally inappropriate. Here's a dose of reality for all of you who can't stand the slightest imperfection in your life. It is not I who has the problem. It is you that has the problem. If dealing with disabled people once in a while is too big

pg.44

a deal for you, too big of an inconvenience for you. Go buy yourself a nice log
cabin for yourself in the mountains or in
the woods. Otherwise, get bent.

When you consider the history of
America, it can be all summed up as the
struggle for equality. It is written in the
Declaration Of Independence "We hold
these truths self evident, that all men are
created equal." (It is written by some his-
torians that the word "men" in the
Declaration Of Independence actually
refers to mankind. Why then, I would
argue, were women not granted the right
to vote until 1920? I would argue further
why were black people denied the right
to vote until 1870?) We may not be perfect, but our country has made great
strides in creating equality for ethnic
minorities, women, people of different
sexual orientations, and of different
faiths.

However, there is one group our
country still needs a lot more done for in
order to make them feel equal; that
group, of course, are disabled Americans.
As of 1990 the Americans With
Disabilities Act states that all public build-
ings must be handicap accessible, but as
with all laws there are legal loopholes.

The legal loophole is that all build-

ings built prior to 1990 are not required
to be handicap accessible and are not
required to upgrade. In addition, private
businesses, restaurants, stores, etc. are
not required to be handicap accessible.
For example if I am a private store locat-
ed on the 2nd story of a strip mall I am
not legally required to put an elevator in.
Putting a side the legal issue though, this
is just bad business. If I am in a wheelchair and I can't access your business, I
am not spending money at your establishment. The goal being of course, the
more people that enter my store or
restaurant the more people there are
spending money. Not having handicap
accessibl prohbits an entire demographic
from spending money at your business.

   With websites there is software
designed to read the text. This was created for visually impaired individuals who
cannot read the words off the monitor. A
problem arises when the software comes
to a graphic it has no way to read. The
W3C, who creates the standard for building websites developed a way around
this. It is called an ALT tag. With the ALT
tag a designer can put a description for
the picture. A person who is not visually
impaired will not see the ALT description

but the text reader will read it. Another
loophole, only government and school
websites are required to have ALT tags
for graphic. Therefore web designers end
up leaving them out of all other websites.

These are just two examples of laws
that need refining in order to make a disabled individual feel more equal. Hopefully
the ADA will continue to create and pass
laws that protect and improve upon the
rights of disabled people to live a fair and
equal life.

You make think I am contradicting
myself by saying I want disabled people
to be treated as equals but I also want all
these laws revised to make our lives easier. You must consider that we are starting from a disadvantage. These laws
don't give us an unfair advantage, if anything they level the playing field so we
can make a contribution and enjoy life
too.

Consider this, I am 7 years old and
have been home from surgery little less
than a year. My left leg is in a brace and
my left arm is in a splint. It is in the dead
of winter and the temperature is -5
degrees, -20 with the wind chill factor. At
the end of the school day I go up to my
first grade teacher.

pg.47

"Could you please help me put on my gloves?" I ask.

"Well if I help you with your gloves, I have to help all the other kids with their gloves too," She answers. "You are no different than any of the rest of the kids, you are responsible for putting on your gloves, not me."

So I went out in the cold without my gloves and waited for the bus. After waiting for 10 or 15 minutes I started losing all feeling in my hands. They turned a shade of dark brownish-red. I went in to see the nurse because I could not bare to be out any longer. The nurse told me another few minutes and I would have gotten frostbite.

(It takes a very special type of moron to turn your back on a physically disabled child, and apathetically send him or her into the cold.)

First of all, "I am not responsible for putting on your gloves," I beg to differ. A teacher's first and foremost job is not that of educator but that of a caregiver. Parents are trusting that teacher with the safety and well being of their children. It is his/her job to make sure that children leave the classroom properly dressed at the end of the day. I am not a lawyer but

pg.48

it sounds to me like what we have here is
a classic case of "depraved indifference".
The definition of depraved indifference
according to
http://www.depravityscale.org/depravi-
ty1.htm is "depraved indifference" means
circumstances which create a grave risk
to human life. Depravity aggravates an
assault charge. Or, even if no physical
injury occurs, depravity warrants a charge
of reckless endangerment" It is gross
negligence to knowingly send out a child
into the cold without gloves. The term
"negligence" means "failure to exercise
the care toward others which a reason-
able"
http://dictionary.law.com/default2.asp?le
tter=N
If I had lost a finger because of her wanting to teach me responsibility my parents
could have sued her personally as well as
my elementary school.

Secondly, "You are no different than
any of the rest of the kids". Are you blind
as well as stupid, I don't see one any
other child here with a splint on his hand
and a brace on his leg. Show me another
child in the classroom who has gone
through brain surgery. The fact is I was
different and it defies both reason and

pg.49

logic not to help out a special needs student put on his gloves.

Abuse comes in all forms and from all places. One place I never thought I would have to worry about abuse is the hospital. Nonetheless in January 2004 that is exactly what I got. After spending 2 days in the ICU (Intensive Care Unit), they decided it was time to move me to a new floor. I had trouble breathing so every so often I would have to ask the nurse or nurses assistant to give me oxygen and suction my nose.

On one occasion I asked the NA (Nurses Assistant) for suction and oxygen and she returned 15 minutes later without it. So I asked again and 15 minutes later she returned again without either. She said, they only had one suction device and one oxygen device on the floor and they were both being used. This, of course was bullshit. So I asked if I could call home which was really pointless since I couldn't talk anyway. Another half hour later the NA returned with the suction device and said, " Here, do it your self, " and threw the instrument at my head.

Why did this happen? Simple; they figured, since he can't talk who is he

going to tell if we treat him like dirt. The
point I am trying to get across is that
mistreatment of disabled Americans happens frequently.

(If the following few paragraphs
sound bitter, pompous, overly critical and
arrogant then you are reading it correctly.)

Recently I went to the DMV to
renew my license. Ah, the DMV where
organization, efficiency, timeliness, and
friendly customer service go to die. I
brought with me a letter stating I had
completed 6 hours of extensive one on
one driving rehabilitation. The letter certi-
fied that I was in fine condition to drive.

I handed the letter to "Fran" at the
DMV, who then informed me I would have
to take a driving test because I am physically disabled. I said to Fran at the DMV,
"Are you aware that this is discrimination?" She was shocked that I would
make such an outlandish accusation.

"I am not discriminating; I make all
the handicapped people take a driving
test. It is my responsibility to assure the
safety of the people on the roads."

"So you make all the handicapped
people take driving tests but the non-
handicapped people don't have to take

pg.51

one?" I asked

"Yes, that's correct." She explained.

"Yet you don't see this as discrimi-nation?"

It seems to me that Fran over at the DMV doesn't have a clear understanding of the word "discrimination". Which is understandable since Fran is in a civil service position. You don't need a college degree to have a civil service position. You must remember when it comes to any kind of government labor force it's usually the incompetent leading the indif-ferent to do the unnecessary. Not to be elitist but garbage men are civil service workers too. I have nothing against garbage men, they are very important to the community but on the other hand it doesn't take a rocket scientist to hawl trash into a truck. So I would put Fran from the DMV's intelligence level some-where between raw sewage and rock. I am quite certain that if you dropped a piano on my head from an extremely high altitude my IQ level would still be much higher than Fran's from the DMV. For those of us who have a mental capacity greater than a slug, lets explore the word "discrimination" shall we?

"Discrimination"- Treatment or con-

sideration based on class or category
rather than individual merit;
So lets review, "I only make all the handicapped people take road tests", is that
discrimination, ah yeah I think so. Is Fran
from the DMV within her legal rights in
making me take the driving test?
Undeniably yes. They're legal in the same
sense that private restaurants in the
South can hang a sign in their windows
that reads "We don't serve Blacks,
Mexicans, Jews, Homosexuals, and other
minorities". It is unmistakenlly legal, but
that doesn't make it right.

If you have ever driven in Florida
you know there are many people who are
driving who shouldn't be. For instance
there is the man who drives down 95
every day with his left blinker on from Ft
Lauderdale to West Palm Beach. There is
the little old lady that sits on a stack of
books and can still barely see above the
steering wheel. There is the lady who evi-
dently doesn't know what her turn signals
are for because she changes lanes on the
highway without using them. Then there
is the elderly gentleman whose eye doctor declared him legally blind but still
managed to get his license renewed at
the DMV. Then this gentleman backed

into a woman in a parking lot but that's
nothing new since a large percent of
Floridians don't look at their mirror when
backing out of a spot anyway.

And last but not least there was the
gentleman who was beginning to back
out of his spot at the doctor's office. I
could see right away he didn't see me so
I honked my horn. The gentleman kept
backing out of his spot so I honked my
horn again. The gentleman keeps backing
up and so I lean on my horn and begin
screaming out my window. Seconds later,
CRASH!!!

The elderly man gets out of his car.

"Sorry I didn't see you." Elderly
gentleman

"What the hell, I was pounding on
my horn !!" I yelled.

"Oh I must not have heard, I am a
bit deaf" said the elderly gentleman.

"Well you shouldn't be driving if
you're a bit deaf Copernicus!!!" I said

All of these people should undoubt-
edly not be driving, but thanks to Fran
there will be less bad "handicapped" drivers in south Florida. If indeed they are
doing it for public safety (which I question since Florida has some of the worst
drivers I've ever seen), then they are dis-

pg.54

criminating for a good reason.
Nonetheless don't lie to me and say your
not discriminating. Try selling "stupid" to
someone else, because I'm not buying.

There was a book written by
Professor J. Philippe called <u>Race,</u>
<u>Evolution, And Behavior</u> published in
1995. This book ranks human beings
according to race on a variety of subjects. Among these subjects are intelligence, athletic ability, and crime. He does
not take into account social/economic
factors in his results. Neither does he
take into account the fact that IQ is
largely biased toward those who were
raised under Western Culture. Would it
surprise you to learn that his findings
were consistent with many typical stereo-
types regarding race? I won't further
gratify Professor Philippe by going into
tremendous details of his book, but there
was one study in particular I'd like to
address. He said statistically those of
Asian descent have the largest heads and
also have statistically the highest IQ's.
According to him those of African
descent typically have the smallest head
size and the lowest IQ's.
His conclusion bigger head-size = bigger brain = more intelligence

pg.55

He then goes on to compare an African person's brain to that of an ape's brain. Well then by all logical accounts elephants should be ruling the world. Elephant's have the largest brain size of any land mammal. For those of you who find Professor Philippe's book shocking, don't be. There were a number of books similar written at the beginning of the 20th Century. It was books like these along with Darwin's Theory of Evolution that inspired Adolph Hitler to write Mein Kampf (My Struggle). Adolf Hitler used ideology of "race" and took it to the extreme: the extermination of 11 million people of "inferior races" (e.g., Jews, Gypsies, Africans, homosexuals, and so forth) and other unspeakable brutalities of the Holocaust.

If you buy into Professor Philippi asinine theories, it is not a gigantic leap to think that those who are physically or mentally disabled are inferior to human beings that are healthy. If you wanted to take this barbaric idea, a step further you could even chart a person's worth according to their disability.

The Chart Of Self Worth	
Healthy adult human	100%
Cancer	90
Diabetic	80%
Blind or Deaf human	70%
physically challenged (Parkison's , Multiple Sclerosis, Muscular Dystrophy, Stroke, brain injury, spinal injury, Quadriplegic etc.	60%
Mobility Impaired (Wheelchair) physically challenged (Parkison's , Multiple Sclerosis, Muscular Dystrophy, Stroke, brain injury, spinal injury, Quadriplegic etc.	50%
Mentally Challenged (Mentally Retarded, Down's Syndrome, Brain Injury, Stroke, Alzheimer, Tourette Syndrome	40%

If you don't find this chart disturbing, might I suggest there is maybe something wrong with you.

People don't expect a whole lot from disabled individuals. If you are disabled this can work both to your advan-

pg.58

tage and disadvantage as well. People will
give you fewer opportunities to prove
yourself, but when the opportunities do
arise seize them, work hard, and I guaran-
tee they will be impressed at your
results.

You can either hold yourself
up to the unrealistic stan-
dards of others, or ignore
them and concentrate on
being happy with yourself as
you are.

J. Jacques ,*Questionable Content webcomic,*
#352, 05-04-05H

H igher Education,And No
Common Sense

The last chapter dealt with prejudice, this chapter deals with a different
kind of prejudice. My senior year of high
school, I was accepted into Purdue
University. I was very excited about going
away because by senior year I hated my
hometown. I felt the whole town was a
bunch of over-privileged money hungry
snobs. My mind was only thinking about
one more year till I get out of this horrible white bread town. I wanted to meet
people, who were different, expand my
horizons so to speak. Be careful what you
wish for. So after the summer of 98 I
packed my bags and my things for

Purdue in West Lafayette Indiana.

I remember the day my parents dropped me off to get me settled in. I got there a week early so I could get myself acclimated to the school. They had a program called Boiler gold rush, where they split up the Freshman into groups, that were each led by one senior. When my parents left I remember sitting for 5 minutes in an empty dorm room the size of a closet that I had to share with a roommate. I thought "now what?" Our RA resident assistant had put our names on all of the rooms so we would get to know each other better. Then I decided to unpack some clothes and things. One of the things I unpacked was a little erasable board for my door so my roommate and I could leave each other messages. I put out the little blue felt tip marker so people could leave us messages as well. After an hour or so of unpacking I decided to go down to the cafeteria to get some lunch.

When I returned from lunch, I noticed from a few doors down from my room that someone had written a message on my message board. I was kind of excited to see what they had written, until I actually saw what they had written.

pg.61

Written in large capital blue letters it said
"GO HOME JEW BOY". I took a paper
towel and scrubbed it off; to be quite
honest I thought they were joking. I figured someone saw the name "Goldstein"
on my door, figured out I must be Jewish
and was just hazing me a little bit. I had
no Idea this was just a small taste of the
things to come.

   A little side note, there were actually 7 or 8 dorms at Purdue one was just
for upperclassman. That left 7 to choose
from. One of the dorms was only for
women so that left 6 to choose from. I
have asthma so I need air conditioning
and only 3 of them had portable air conditioning units. Out of the three dorms I
had left to choose from mine was known
to have the best food. (It really was.
There is a thing known as the Freshman
15, because freshmen tend to eat too
much at the buffet style cafeterias. They
stamp your card and then it's all you can
eat. I actually put on the Freshman 40.
When I went home for the holidays in
December I was the heaviest I ever was in
my entire life.) So that was how I ended
up at Shreve Hall. What I didn't know was
that Shreve Hall was also considered the
Bible dorm. I found that out a tad too

late. Also worth noting is that Purdue had more than one church, but not one synagogue. So on Friday nights we went to the Hillel for Shabbat dinner and to pray. People had shattered the windows of our Hillel by throwing a rock through several times through the years so they had to put bullet proof glass in.

My roommate was a devout Christian but I got along with him fine and of course he got along with all the religious people on my floor fine. I remember my first Sunday at the dorm my roommate was getting ready to go to church, when a few of the guys from my floor knocked on my door. My roommate answered it, exchanged greetings, and then the religious leader from the floor said to me, "well aren't you going to come with us?"

I said "no"

Which he of course followed with a "why not?"

I wanted to say "none of your damn business," but I managed to keep it under control. "I don't go to church," I explained.

Well of course he wasn't going to let it go that easy "Why not?" he asked again. The rest of the group kept quiet

during my inquisition, including my roommate.

"I am Jewish I don't go to temple," I
said my voice beginning to rise in frustra-
tion.

"What is that, some kind of new
color?" He asked.

It took me a few seconds to realize
what he was asking. He must have
thought I said bluish, as in I am wearing a
bluish sweater. I was kind of in a state of
shock because I had never met someone
who didn't know what a Jew was.

You mean you don't know what a
Jew is? Did you grow up in a cave?" I
asked mockingly. Some of these people
that went to Purdue grew up in extremely
small town and had never been out of the
state of Indiana. I knew a girl whose graduating class in high school consisted of
only 4 people. They all went to the prom
as a group because they had two boys
and two girls. Another guy told me his
entire town had only one traffic light.
Point being, these were not the worldliest
people in the world. Many admitted their
house did not have a television.

"No, I don't" He snapped back.

"It is another religion," I stated
shaking my head like this was self-appar-

pg.64

ent.

"What do you mean, another religion?" He asked.

"You know what, I'll explain it to you another time, you will be late for church," I said not wanting to have this discussion any longer.

After that, the entire group would just blandly pretend I didn't exist. They wouldn't say as much as hello to me. They would knock on my door when I was studying; when I would answer they would only say, "Where's Jeffrey?" (Referring to my roommate). Occasionally, I left my door open during the day and they would just walk right in, take a look around for Jeffrey and then leave without saying a word to me. This was definitely something I was not used to. In my hometown in the northern suburbs of Chicago, no one cared what religion you were. To be quiet honest I had more non-Jewish friend's growing up then I had Jewish one's. Of course, my hometown was also 65 percent Jewish. Here in West Lafayette In. half the people did not know what a Jew was and more than that had never met one.

The problems were not just limited to the dorms. My very first English class

pg.65

another student walked up to me.
Goldstein, Goldstein.." He said as if pon-
dering a great question. Then he said to
me "Is you Jewish?" I had never heard
the English language so thoroughly
butchered (especially in an English class!).

I thought oh no here we go again.
"Yes, I is Jewish" I answered back lethar-
gically.

"You know Jerry Springer is Jewish."
Not knowing where he was going with
this I wore an inquisitive dumbfounded
expression on my face. "That's so cool,
hey everyone this guys just like
Springer," He continued.

I could have busted a gut laughing
at this guy but instead it took all my
powers of concentration to maintain my
composure. I decided I was going to have
some fun at this fool's expense.

"Indeed, all of us Jews are exactly
like Springer" I said trying my best to
maintain a serious look on my face.
"In fact, he's our leader " I explained to
him slowly, like an adult explaining something to a small child. (Funny part is,
out of all the famous Jews there
have been throughout American history, Einstein, not to mention all the
Jewish actors and actresses and

pg.66

comedians. The two Jews that people associated with me the most
were Jerry Springer and Howard
Stern. My personality is neither
remotely similar to either omd.)

Just when I thought the conversation couldn't possibly get any more assi-
nine then it already was, a girl in the cor-
ner lowered the bar a bit more.

"You're Jewish?" She asked.

"Yes, didn't we just establish that
30 seconds ago" I responded with a
chuckle.

"Where are you from?" She asked.
"Chicago" I answered quickly without a
thought.
"You know I have a Jewish friend in
Chicago; his name is Ben. Do you know
him?", She asked, very sincerely.
"Oh, Jewish Ben, Ben the Jew as we call
him in Chicago. Sure everyone knows Ben
the Jew." I said mockingly.
"Are you making fun of me?" She asked.
I thought, gee your pretty quick
Copernicus, didn't need Sherlock Holmes
to solve that mystery for you, did ya? At
least she was smart enough to understand I was being sarcastic and having
fun at her expense. I can't say the same
for other people I met at Purdue.

pg.67

One day, the Gideon's came to
town. I had no idea what a Gideon even
was. The Gideon's as to my understanding were a group of old men that go
around passing bibles. All day long as I
was walking to and from my classes
these Gideon's shouted at me "open your
heart to Jesus Christ", "Christ died for
your sins", "The bible has all the answers
you need". They would even follow you if
you tried to walk past them. They were
annoying.

Then one of them unzipped my bag
as I was walking away from him. Then he
slipped a bible inside my bag. I came
close to chucking it at him but remembered it was a sacred document to many
people and choose to hand it to him
instead.

"Don't you want to hear the sweet
words of Jesus Christ?"

"No thanks" I said.

"But Jesus loves you"

"That's great, still don't want a
bible," I said
(Still following me to class,) "Jesus is
your lord and savior"

Then I got annoyed, "Ya know what I
worship the Devil!!" I yelled in the most
demonic voice I could muster. That shut

him up. Turned his face white like a bed
sheet too. I didn't want to be mean but
he pushed me to it.
During my break I approached one of
these Gideon's.

"What is your purpose in being
here?" I asked.

"We want to help people by spreading the words of the lord." He answered

"If you really want to help people
you should donate time at a soup
kitchen, or work for a charity," I said. I
might as well have been speaking to a
wall; it would have had the same effect.

When I finally went back to my dorm
for lunch I was thoroughly annoyed. I said
to a guy at my table, " Can you believe
those Gideons? They have been harassing
me all day long!"

After lunch I went back to my dorm
room to work on an art project. Minutes
after I got to the room I get a phone call.
It was one of the guys I had eaten lunch
with. He asked if he could come up to my
room and I told him all right. I unlocked
my door so he would be able to come in
without interrupting me from doing my
art project. When I am working on something important I tune out everything
else. So when he showed up I just yelled,

pg.69

"The Door is open". I didn't even look up
or I would have noticed he was carrying a
bible with him.

"Brad" he said, "I'd like to discuss
the Gideons with you."

"What's to discuss?" I asked looking
up "Oh no, is that a bible?" I asked
annoyed.

"Brad, I am worried about you," He
said with a tone of concern in his voice.

"And why is that?" I asked mildly
amused.
"Because you don't follow the teachings
of Jesus, I don't want your soul to go to
hell," He said very seriously.

It was then I decided I would have
fun at this guy's expense. "Actually I am

from Chicago so the heat will be a nice
change" I said jokingly. Of course he took

pg.70

me seriously.

"But you will be tortured for eternity!" He said almost pleadingly.

"Eh, after a while I'll get used to it," I said ever so nonchalantly. "If you had ever been to my home town you would see Hell is a step up."

"Really?" He asked his voice filled with alarm.

"No, I'm making fun of you, you shmuck. You're not going to successfully convert me, so either move on to a new subject or leave my room."

"But Jesus loves you"

"Sorry never met the guy" I responded

"Okay Brad, I can see I'm not getting through to you. I see you like art," he said, "Do you mind if I draw something"

"Knock yourself out," I answered. At this point I had submersed all my mental energy into my art project once again. A minute later he showed me his drawing. It was a cross with a little stick figure on the left and another one on top.

"This is a map on how to get to heaven," He explained. The figure on the left is you and the figure on the top is Jesus Christ and to the right is the kingdom of heaven.

At

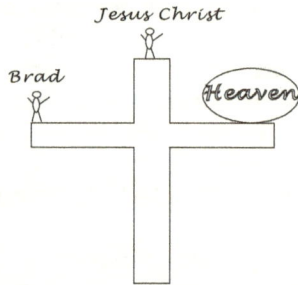

this point I was trying hard not to
explode into a fit of laughter. Then he
drew a curvy line connecting all three.
"You see Brad, the only way into heaven
is to go through Jesus Christ. He
explained this patronizingly as if he was
talking to a four year old.
I really couldn't help myself. "May I borrow your pen for a minute?" I asked.

"Sure," he replied.

"Okay catch this, what if we take
highway 95 and get off at exit 30?" I
asked. "Would that get me into heaven?"
I continued.

"No Brad, there is no highway to
heaven." He explained.

"Sure there is; it was a T.V show in
the 70's" I argued

(In actuality I drew 3 different non-

pg.72

sense path scenarios to heaven. One
involved a helicopter and a parachute, the

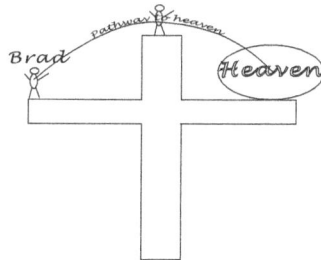

other drill and mountain climbing equipment)

It was at this point that the guy
ceased to be amusing and was starting to
get on my nerves.

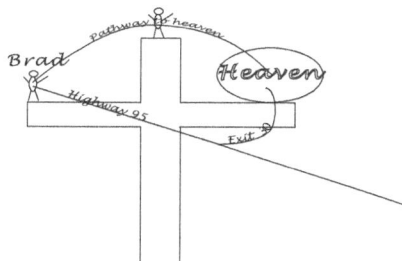

"Okay buddy you're getting on my
nerves. You have to the count of 5 to

pg.73

get out of my room or I'll throw you out,"
I said. I only got to the count of 2 before
he left.

One night after returning to the
dorm from exercising at the rec. center, I
happened to over hear a conversation.
(Actually I over heard the conversation because I am a nosy S.O.B, but
that's getting bogged down into
specifics.)

"I'm telling you, there was never any
dinosaurs!" I heard Jon yelling.

I thought I probably should mind my
own business and stay out of this intellectually stimulating debate (sarcastic);
but what fun would that be?

So I went into the room where I
heard this discussion taking place.
"Jon, no if there were Dinosaurs before
the existence of man they would have
been written about in the bible," he said

"No Jon, there were never any D-R-
A-G-O-N-S; (I said slowly to empha-
size the distinction and impact the
fact that I was talking to a moron)
dinosaurs on the other hand did exist. I
can see how someone with your limited
intelligence might get the two confused,"
I said mockingly.

"Where did you come from?" Jon

snapped.

"I was down the hall and I heard stu-
pidity coming from this room, so I figured
it was you," I declared smugly.

"If there were dinosaurs before the
existence of man, they would have been
written about in the bible," Jon explained.

"How can you argue against scientif-
ic fact, what about those gigantic bones
they have at the museums, I believe
those are dinosaur bones," I stated in my
"duh" voice, as if that should be obvious.

"And how do you know those bones
didn't belong to a different animal?" Jon
shouted.

"What, like a 100 foot dog perhaps?" I asked inquisitively. "You know
they do carbon dating on those bones to
prove how far back they go." I replied

"And how do you know they do that
carbon dating correctly?" Jon Inquired

It was at about this point I realized
it didn't matter what I said, because you
can't have a logical conversation with
someone who has no logic and reasoning
skills. I might as well be debating with a
monkey, it would have the same effect.

When you are living on a college
campus, there are only two ways off the
campus public transportation or you hitch

pg.75

a ride. If you know someone who lives on your floor that has a car, you want to make that person your friend. Unfortunately for me, the only one who lived on my floor that had a car was Jon.

So if I wanted a ride into town or to the mall I had to bite my tongue less I say something to offend him. Of course Jon wasn't going to make that easy for me. On one occasion I asked him if I could have a ride to the grocery store.

"Why, what do you need, that you can't get at the campus grocery store?" He asked, as if that was any of his business.

Trying not to get upset, "I wanted to get some bagels" I said calmly.

"What's with you Jews and bagels?" He asked innocently.

The only other time I asked Jon for a ride was when he and my roommate were going to the mall. Again being the nisy fuck that he is, he asked the same question.

"Why what do you need at the mall?" He asked.

I took a deep breath, rolled my eyes exhaled and then said "I want to buy a Barbara Streisand CD,"

To which he responded with of

course "What's with you Jews and Barbara Streisand?"

The guy who lived next door to me had his family visiting quite often. His younger brother who I am guessing was around 11 was always bored out of his mind. So I would let him play games on my computer while his family was next door.

On one occasion I was studying while snacking on some matzo (unleavened bread that came from when the Jews were escaping from Egypt.) The kid asked me what I was eating and I explained what it was. He asked if he could have a piece and I said sure. After a half hour or so of playing video games on my computer he returned to his brother's room, still eating the matzo. When his family saw him eating the unrecognizable food they freaked.

"What the hell are you eating?" Yelled his mother.

"It's called matzo," explained the child to his mother.

"I don't care what it's called" she yelled as she smacked the matzo out of his hand, "You don't eat anything unless I say so."

"It is just unleavened bread," I said

trying to smooth things over.

His parents just glared at me, and I went back to my room. I never figure out why they got so angry, perhaps they thought they would have to re-baptize their son after eating the "Jew Food". That was the last time the boy knocked on my door to play video games. I'm guessing that was his parent's decision and not his.

Jon came up to me one Sunday morning with his bible group.

"Do you want to come to church with us?" He asked

"Haven't we had this discussion before Jon?," I Inquired.

"Why don't you just try going once, maybe you will like it," he whined.

"Tell you what, I'll go to church with you today if you go to Synagogue with me next friday evening," I bargained.

"Oh I can't do that, that's complete-ly different," he said.

At which point my roomate said "How's that different?" That shut him up.

It seems to me that trying to force-ably convert someone is entirely un-Chrishtian. Correct me if I'm wrong but wasn't it Jesus himself who said "Let he who is without sin cast the first stone",

pg.78

"Judge not less you be judged yourself".
In otherwords don't go looking to critize
other people. Religion is a perssonel relationship between a person and God and
should not be influenced by those outside
of the family.

Nonetheless, that was life my
freshman year of college. I know I have
painted a pretty dark picture of what life
was like my freshman year but I had actually had more friends in the one year at
Purdue than the other three and half
years I spent at the private college in
Chicago. In fact no matter what time it
was I always had people to hang out with.
The people that bombarded me with anti-
Semetic commentary and tried to convert
me were in the minority, not the majority.
In my next 3 and half years at Columbia
College, finding friendly people to hang
out with would be far more difficult. The
reason I left Purdue had nothing to do
with their Holier than thou attitude of the
people in my classes or dorm. At the time
I thought I was making the right decision.
Later I realized I was wrong.

There will always be a part, and
always a very large part of every
community, that have no care but
for themselves, and whose care for
themselves reaches little further
than impatience of immediate pain,
and eagerness for the nearest good.

Samuel Johnson (1709 - 1784)

T HE GOOD SAMARATAN WHERE ART THOU?

If something happens to you, you
fall, you have an accident, you feel ill, or
there is some other form of emergency,
you call on your telephone or cell phone
for help. What if you can't get to a phone

pg.80

or your cell phone's battery goes dead or
looses service. Suppose you pass out on
the sidewalk from sunstroke, or an allergic
reaction causes you to stop breathing.
What if you suffer a heart attack, seizure
or stroke? Who will help you then? If you
answered a good samaritan, then the following story might have you rethink your
answer.

When I was 15, the summer after
my freshman year of high school, my parents took a trip to Las Vegas. One hot
day I decided to take out my bike for a
ride. I had no destination planned, just
out to get some exercise on a hot summer afternoon. I took a ride past a park a
five minute drive from my house, when
some punk adolescent with baggy jean
shorts rode his dirt bike up beside me,
and took out a squirt gun and sprayed
what I assumed was water in my eyes.
Being that it was hot I decided to just
continue riding, thinking the sun would
soon dry up my face. It took me about a
minute to realize it was not water he
sprayed at all. The liquid burned my eyes
and the skin on my face. On pure reflex I
started to rub my eyes, which probably
made it worse not better.
 I started to chase after the degenerate

on my bike. He rode his bike into a local
strip mall and disappeared into the crowd.
I would have followed him except at this
point my eyes were burning so badly that
my vision was becoming severely compro-
mised. My tear ducts were producing so
many tears that my vision began to blur. I
thought if I was to ride into the strip mall
I would surely hit someone with my bike
or worse yet get hit by a car.

So I rode my bike back to the park.
By this time I was franticly rubbing my
eyes. The skin on my face was all red and
blotchy. I began rubbing my eyes with
one hand and waving my arm with the
other hoping a car would stop and ask me
what was wrong. Finally a jogger passed
by me.

I yelled, "Sir can you help me.." but
the jogger didn't stop, he just kept on
jogging. A few minutes later another jogger came by.

Again I yelled "Sir can you help me?
Some kid sprayed mace in my eyes."

"There's a water fountain by the
playground," He answered. "Why don't
you try to wash your eyes out there?" he
said, as his voice faded as he resumed
jogging.

So I went to the water fountain and

spent a few minutes trying to rinse the
mace or pepper spray out of my eyes. No
such luck, my eyes still burned as they
did before. It was then I spotted a lady
on the playground supervising her kids.

I said "Excuse me, can you help me?
Some kid sprayed mace in my eyes."

The woman said, "I'd let you use my
cell phone but I am all out of free minutes and it is real expensive if you call
now"

So I rode my bike home half blind,
squinting to see for 3 miles. In certain
area where the sidewalk thinned I had to
walk my bike because I was afraid I'd ride
off the path. When I got home I rushed to
the bathroom again to wash my eyes,
and then called my aunt to take me to
the hospital.

I have told this story a few times and
the first question I always get is what kind
of degenerate gets kicks of spraying pepper spray into the eyes of complete
strangers? To be quite frank, I don't know.
Perhaps his mother didn't show him
enough attention growing up, maybe his
father abused him, or his mother was sniff-
ing crack when she was pregnant with
him. The other question is what kind of
dumb-asses allows their son access to a

bottle of mace or pepper spray? I don't
have an answer for either of these questions and quite honestly don't care either.
My biggest beef is not with the demented,
twisted child but with the people at the
park who would not take the time to help
a fellow human being.

You may be wondering what if anything this all has to do with being disabled.
First of all, if you read my prologue you
would know this whole book is not about
being disabled. However there is a connection. Right now, I am mute. If I fall or
get hurt I cannot pick up a cell phone
and call for help. If I fall at home I have a
button on a necklace I wear that will alert
people that I am hurt or injured. However,
if I am away from home and something
happens that button will not function.

About four months ago I was at a
strip mall, and bent down to pick up my
keys, which I had dropped. When I tried
to get back up, my leg gave out and I
landed hard on my knee. I was not
though, I figured I was in the middle of a
crowded strip mall and that sooner or
later a friendly, considerate person will
offer me assistance. Indeed people did
walk right up to me and then right by me,
in fact a man got into his car not 12 feet

away from me. It occurred to me after 15
minutes that if I was waiting for someone
to help me I might be waiting quite a
while. So I crawled on my hands and
knees like an infant towards a ledge
where a bunch of plants were. It was
maybe 8 feet away from me. Then I used
the ledge to prop myself back up to a
standing position. By this time my legs
were scraped and bruised and the shorts I
wore were stained with blood. All this and
I still had a good mile yet to walk home.

Imagine the following scenario:
You're taking a walk and discover a
human being lying unconscious on the
sidewalk in front of you. You kneel down
to see if the person is still breathing; he is
not. You check his pulse, and yes his heart
is still beating. You call for help on your cell
phone and begin administering CPR. The
paramedics arrive and the victim is rushed
to the hospital. Congratulations, you just
saved a human life. Weeks later the victim
shows up at your place of work.

How are you feeling?" You ask.

Much better he responds, but while
you were giving me CPR you fractured
one of my ribs, and I am suing you for
damages.

The previous example would make

anyone reluctant to help a person in
need. To go through the trouble of saving
a perfect strangers life, and then finding
out that not only isn't the person grateful,
but he is suing you for your efforts. I don't
know about you, but I would take a fractured rib over not breathing any day of
the week. It is lawsuits like this that are one
of the reasons why people are weary
about helping another in need.

As a result the states passed Good
Samaritan Laws protecting those who act
in good faith to save another human
being. The following is the a copy of the
Florida Good Samaritan Laws:
"Any person, including those licensed to
practice medicine, who gratuitously and in
good faith renders emergency care or
treatment either in direct response to
emergency situations related to and aris-
ing out of a state of emergency which
has been declared pursuant to s. 252.36
or at the scene of an emergency outside
of a hospital, doctor's office, or other
place having proper medical equipment,
without objection of the injured victim or
victims thereof, shall not be held liable
for any civil damages as a result of such
care or treatment or as a result of any
act or failure to act in providing or

arranging further medical treatment
where the person acts as an ordinary rea-
sonably prudent person would have acted
under the same or similar circumstances."
(Found on http://www.floridamalprac-
tice.com/stat768.13.htm)

These laws vary from state to state
but the underlining premise is the same.
Any person who in good faith acts in helping another should not be held liable for
damages caused by their actions.

Another reason people fail to act is
fear of disease transmitted by blood or
saliva. It is a fear that I feel is valid which is
why I keep a CPR mask in my glove com-
partment. It is a little piece of plastic that
folds over the person face; you either
breathe through a tube or tiny holes in the
plastic. Even if
you don't know
CPR, there is no
reason why
you can't call
911 on your cell
phone, or
knock on the
door of a near-
by house or
business and
have them

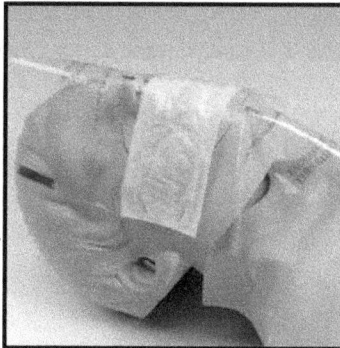

call.

The other reason which makes no sense to me at all, is people feel they are too busy to help or simply don't care. It's not my problem why should I help?" During one of my classes in college my professor instructed the class that if they were ever being attacked to yell, fire" rather than help or rape. In terms of statistics, it is more likely that a person will come to your aid if you yell fire than rape or help. There is a very simple reason for this; when you yell help or rape that tells others that you are in danger. If they don't act they remain safe. In contrast, if you yell fire, people think that their safety is being threatened and will want to see how far away from the fire they are. This is a sad commentary on contemporary American life.

The following are steps you can take to maximize your chances of being helped should the unthinkable happen. These apply to both disabled and non-disabled people:

1. Keep in your wallet or purse a card listing the name of someone to contact in case of an emergency along with his or her phone number.

2. On the card list what medications you are currentlytaking along with any medications you are allergic too. When paramedics arrive on the sceen they have no way of knowing your medical history and could possibly inject you with medications you are allergic to. That will only make a bad situation worse, possibly fatal.

3. If you are a pedestrian at night, stick to streets that are well lit so you are more likely to be seen in the unlikely event of an emergency.

4. Do not take short cuts through alleys unless another traveler accompanies you.

5. Don't let your kids ride their bikes or skateboards in the empty parking lots of businesses during the weekend. If something happens nobody will spot your child until the next business day.

6. Stick to streets that have heavy pedestrian traffic; your chances of someone helping you are much greater.

It's a recession when
your
neighbor loses his job;
it's a depression when
you lose yours.

**Harry S Truman (1884 - 1972) ,in
The Observer, April 13, 1958**

Finding A Job Is
The Hardest Job Of
All
(and the pay is lousy)

There were many uncertainties,
growing up with a disability, . Would my
hand get better? Would I ever marry or
have children? There was no doubt in my
mind, however, that whatever I did for a
living, I would be successful. There was a

pg.91

time not long ago in America's history
where if you went to an accredited college or university and received a degree,
you could then venture out into the world
of business and begin a career. I use the
word "career" rather than job for an obvious reason and there is a big difference. I
am not referring to salary, or even pres-
tige. Any body can get a job, just look
for a "help wanted" sign" in any store
inside a mall or strip mall, fast food joint,
or grocery store. If you look in the dictionary you will find careers defined as
the following:
noun;
1.   a job or occupation regarded as
a long-term or lifelong activity
2.   somebody's progress in a chosen profession or during that person's working life
3.   the general path or progress
taken by somebody or something
4.   a rushing onward while lurching
or swaying
adj.
1.   trained for and expecting to
work in a particular occupation for
an entire working life rather than

briefly
Encarta® World English Dictionary ©
1999 Microsoft Corporation.
As the number of college graduates
increases each year, it's becoming more
and more competitive.

I graduated high school in 97.
Before I even began applying to colleges
my junior year in school, I did two things.
First I took that aptitude test that tells
you what kind of job you'd be good for.
Second I got a list of all the professions
rated by earning potential and growing
fields. Both Graphic Design and Web
Design were listed in the top 10 in both
lists.

Being that I was partially disabled I
was more limited in choices than your
average college student but Graphic
Design and Web design were both in the
realm of things I was physically capable of
doing. Next I searched for colleges that
offered Graphic Design as a major. This
led me to Purdue University in West
Lafayette, Indiana (for more on my
time at Purdue see my chapter
regarding anti-Semitism). At the end
of my freshman year I found an animation

pg.93

course that I was interested in taking
next fall, unfortunately it was in another
department. As was my understanding at
the time, there were only two things that
could prevent you from taking a class.
One, the class is full, and two you don't
have the prerequisites to the class. Since
the class had no prerequisites I thought I
could sign up for the class. (I'll go into
more detail on this in a following
chapter.) Suffice it to say, they would
not allow me to take the course and told
me I would have to wait at least a year
before I could take it. So I began looking
at other colleges and universities.
Eventually I would enroll at Columbia
College in Chicago.

Columbia College had every class I
could ever want to take and then some.
At first I had double majored in Graphic
Design and Animation. Before long I realized I didn't have the skill to be a traditional animator and would switch majors
yet again. My final major was Interactive
Multimedia (Animation for the web), with
a minor in Graphic Design. I figured this
way I'd have information on all three and
make me more marketable. It took me

longer than 4 years to graduate because
of switching schools and switching
majors. The next 3 and half years were
plagued with bad roommates, (a topic for
another book perhaps) and lots of hard
work.

Rather than wait till I graduated I
decided to get an early start on sending
out resumes. I began doing so six months
prior to graduating. An Interesting fact,
was at this time both Graphic Design and
Web Design were now at the bottom of
the job list in terms of earning potential
and growth. I had known several people
who had chosen not to go to college and
instead taught themselves the programs
and languages they saw companies were
looking for. These people beat the dot
com. rush and received jobs before these
companies maxed out. In three months I
had E-mailed, Faxed and Mailed over fifteen hundred resumes without a single
response or interview.   Everyday I
searched the want ads, and websites like
jobfinder, monster, and employment911.
One generality I began noticing was that
the majority of the ads said "must have 5
years experience", "must have 8 years

pg.95

experience", "must have 10 years experience". I saw one ad that said must have
20 years web experience to which I wrote
the following letter:

Dear Dumb asses,

The World Wide Web has not even
been around 20 years, you morons. Next
time you place an ad in the Newspaper
try doing some research first assholes!!!

Best Regards,

Brad Goldstein

I wonder why they never replied?
Nonetheless, this presented a definite
problem. How do you get experience
when no one is willing to give you a job?
From a business perspective it makes
perfect sense. Leo Burnett is one of the
largest graphic design companies in the
world. Their clientele includes:
Kellogg's, Procter & Gamble, Philip Morris,
H.J. Heinz, Fiat, Visa, McDonald's, Kraft
Foods, Hallmark, Morgan Stanley, Diageo,
and Walt Disney. When I began my job
search the reports were the company had
laid off a percentage of their employees.
The good news was with Leo Burnett on
their resume they were easily hired else-
where, the bad news these companies

couldn't afford to pay them what Leo
Burnett paid them, so they had to take a
salary decrease. If you put yourself in the
Graphic Design Companies shoes, whom
would you rather hire? A young adult who
is straight out of college, that you will
have to train or pay slightly higher or a
former employee of Leo Burnett who has
10 years under his belt. I understand the
logic and economics of it, but still doesn't
make my life any easier.

When all else fails, Intern
So then the question is how do you
get experience when no one is willing to
give you a job? So I went to my guidance
counselor to ask that very question. The
answer they gave, "do an internship." So I
went to the head of my department and
told them I wanted to do an internship.
They said sure thing, you just need to
give us $400.00. The school wants you
to pay because you're receiving school
credits for doing the internship. I didn't
need the credits, and furthermore didn't
have $400.00. Even if I had $400.00 I
was not about to waste it on credits I
didn't need. I didn't mind working for
free, but being $400.00 in the hole to

work didn't make sense. So the school
gave me a list of companies that provide
internships, but basically told me that
was all the help they would provide me.

I knew a little bit about internships
from friends of mine, and a lot of what I
heard wasn't good. I was told stories
where students worked internships where
all they did was sweep floors, make coffee, make copies, and get everyone's
lunch. I have no problem with paying my
dues or starting at the bottom but it is
not enough to put on a resume, that you
interned with a company. You also have
to list what you did for that company.
You can't put on a resume that you
swept floors, made coffee, and picked up
lunches. Sure you can lie on a resume but
in my field if you say you worked on a
project, when your interviewed they're
going to want to see it.

So to avoid this problem, I went to
see the head of the company before I
even began my internship to work out
the details. They had some "grunt" work
that they wanted me to do before I
began working on their website. The
"grunt" work entailed dubbing or making

pg.98

copies of their tapes and digitizing and
cleaning up old photographs. The dubbing
process is mind numbingly boring, it
entails putting one tape in a VCR and
pressing play and putting another tape in
the other VCR and pressing record. The
digitizing photographs were a bit more
complex because it involved scanning in
some photographs, adjusting bright-
ness/contrast, and cleaning up dust and
scratches. However I was assured that
when I completed these two tasks I would
begin the more meaty projects. Which
brings me to probably the only advice
you will get from me this chapter and
that is:
GET IT IN WRITING!!!
GET IT IN WRITING!!!
GET IT IN WRITING!!!
"What's that you say?"
GET IT IN WRITING!!!
GET IT IN WRITING!!!
GET IT IN WRITING!!!
"I'm sorry one more time, I wasn't paying
attention."
GET IT IN WRITING!!!
GET IT IN WRITING!!!
GET IT IN WRITING!!!

pg.99

People's words arn't usually worth shit. In reality verbal contracts are legally binding, but proving them without a third party present is near impossible. You get into a whole he said; she said that really won't get you anywhere. So whenever you reach an agreement with someone from the time you enter college and for the rest of you life Always Get It In Writing!

I only had three months to intern for this company. They had over 400 tapes each 4 hours long that needed to be dubbed and they had thousands of photographs that needed to be digitized and cleaned up. It didn't take me long to realize I would never have a chance to work on their companies website. When the 3 months were over I had nothing to put on my resume and no work I could show in my portfolio.

It's not what you know; it's who you know

This is certainly true if you have the right connections. I knew students who after they graduated high school, their mommy and daddy set them up with a cushy position within their company. Of

course they had no experience and were
under qualified for the positions they
were offered, but that doesn't matter
when your daddy is president of the company. These young adults who received
"C's" and "D's" in high school are now
making a hundred grand a year. My problem was I didn't know anybody.

So I went back to my guidance counselor for more advice. She suggested I
begin networking. So I spent a hundred
dollars printing up business cards and
handed them out to people wherever I
went. I passed out business cards at wed-
dings, bar and bat mitzvahs, and just
about every place you could imagine. I
joined the Multimedia users group in
Chicago. The problem with the users
group was the majority of them were
unemployed too. I went to trade shows;
conventions anywhere where there were
people. Not one job offer, not one phone
call.

About this time I had nearly wiped
out my savings account paying for my
apartment. To make matters worse my
parents informed me that they were moving to Florida and if I didn't find a way to

pay for my apartment in 5 months I'd
have to move with them. I tried desperately to find any job, just so I could
remain in Chicago. Most jobs I interviewed
for in retail or otherwise now told me
that I was overqualified for their positions. The only jobs that I could find barely covered my food and rent without letting me put away anything in my savings.
So at the end of 5 months I packed up
my things, and I moved to Florida with
my mother and father.

For three months I faxed out resumes
to Graphic Design and Web Design companies. I sent out another two thousand
resumes with cover letters and all I
received was rejection letters. I got a full-
time job at Brookstone across the street
from where I lived. During the time I
worked I still called companies, and faxed
and E-mailed resumes. One day I was calling to follow up on a resume and the man
on the phone said they used me on a trial
basis. He said to come in Monday ready
to work. So Monday I came in and immediately went in to see the owner to intro-
duce myself. My conversation went something like this:

pg.102

"Hello sir, I am Brad Goldstein. I am supposed to start today. Nice to meet you." I said extending my arm to shake his hand.

"Nice to meet you too... hey what's wrong with your left hand?"

"Oh it's a long story, it doesn't work too well, but my right hand works fine."

"Well I'm sorry to waste your time, but you can't work here if your disabled."

"Yeah, that's funny," I said laughing.

"No, I'm serious, Why would I hire you, when I can hire someone with two perfectly good hands?"

I couldn't believe what I was hearing. Sad and defeated I took the elevator down and walked out to the parking lot. I called my family on my cell phone to tell them what had happened. All of a sudden a light went on inside my head. He can't do that, that's discrimination. I took the elevator back up and marched into his office.

"You know what you said to me was discrimination, and I am going to sue you for every penny you have!"

I stormed out with the man following right behind me. "Brad, look I'm sorry to

pg.103

waste your time. Why don't you take a
weeks pay for your troubles and we will
forget all of this," He said taking out his
checkbook.

"No, I want to sue your ass, you
fucking prick! When I am done with you I
will own your company!" I screamed

If he wanted someone who could
type quickly, he could have just administered a typing test and if I failed said,
"I'm sorry you type to slow". However, he
did not, he just assumed I typed slowly
by the looks of my hand. I filed a com-
plaint with the equal employment agency.
The first question they asked me was,
"Does he have more than 15 employees?" I didn't know it at the time but a
company that has 15 or less employees
is considered a "private company". Even
if the building they reside in is a public
building. "Private Companies", can openly
discriminate against anyone they want.
This means he can say to an applicant
"We don't hire disabled people here",
"We don't hire Jews here", "We don't hire
blacks here" and there is nothing you can
do about it.

When you go to fill out an application

now, you may notice a disclaimer written on it that says this:

This company is an equal opportunity employer. We do not discriminate against age, race, gender, sexual orientation, or religion. BULL SHIT!!! The fact remains, that companies can discriminate for what ever reason they want. All they have to tell you is they had a better applicant. Unless you have proof, there is not a thing you can do about it.

As I sit here typing this chapter, it has been four years since I graduated the college. Sure, I'm not the only one I know who graduated college and couldn't find work. However it is different for me, because I am disabled. I can't wait tables, I can't lift boxes, and I can't do telemarketing. In the time I graduated I went to my college and to the state employment agencies but neither has gotten any results. I don't offer any advice in this chapter, because I have none to give. In fact, if I offered advice I would have to be the world's biggest hypocrite. The fact is the state, rather pay me social security and have me sit here like an old, useless record collection gathering dust, than help me get a job.

I can win an argument on any topic, against any opponent. People know this, and steer clear of me at parties. Often, as a sign of their great respect, they don't even invite me.

Dave Barry (1947 -)

Being a Control Freak

And

Learning to Let The Small Things Slide

Once upon a time there lived a very easygoing child, then life plagued him with a tumor and whole mess of crap happened to him. The control freak was born. In my life I have had many things happen to me, that were completely out of my control. So I decided I would attempt to take control of every aspect of my life that was within my grasp.

pg.107

I spoke of Doctor Phil in my
Prologue. In doctor Phil's book Life
Strategies there is a chapter titled "We
teach people how to treat us". To summarize the chapter, if someone treats
you like crap, and you don't do or say
anything about it. They will continue to
treat you like crap. I adopted this philoso-
phy long before Dr. Phil hit the shelves at
the bookstore. I realized very early on
that life had left me at a disadvantage.
So, I overcompensated by being
assertive. At some point I surpassed
assertive and went on to become aggres-
sive. The following list of words describes
this aspect of my personality: brash,
abrasive, argumentative, obnoxious, tena-
cious, over zealous, annoying, uncompro-
mising, loud, and bossy. To make matters
worse adopting this attitude often got
me what I wanted. In school if I worked
on a group project, it was understood
that I was the group leader. On one occasion a teacher passed out our grades for
a project and a member of group said,

"B– we deserve better than a B–,
Brad go argue with the teacher".

To which I replied, "Why should I

pg.108

argue with the teacher?"

"Because your good at it"

I hated group projects, if I couldn't do things the way I wanted I just assume work alone.

I loved to argue. It didn't have to be about something important; I argued because I enjoyed it. I argued with my classmates, my teachers and my bosses. I never really realized how bad I was. It's not enough to be assertive; it's knowing when to assert yourself and how to do so tactfully. All through growing up I had a problem with authority. In my mind they were trying to take away my control, which presented a problem to me.

In high school I took CAD class (Computer Aided Drafting). Half the projects were on the computer; the other half was by hand. The computer projects I got an A on every one of them. The hand projects I failed every one of them. Due to my disabled left hand I could not hold the ruler straight and I could not cut straight. My projects came out jagged and crooked. My teacher down graded my projects because they were not neat. I explained to him that this was not in my control but it fell on deaf ears. I made the analogy; it's like a gym teacher telling a student who is in a wheelchair you're going to mark down his grade because he could not run the half-mile in class.

To which he said, "My left leg doesn't work that well, but I still walk on it everyday."

This pissed me off. "You know I don't know anything about your disability and you don't know anything about mine so don't go making assumptions, that you know what it's like to be in my shoes because you don't. You know when you go ASSUMING…."

"Yeah, yeah, I make an ass out of U and Me"

"No actually that wasn't what I was going to say. You make a HUGE ASS out of yourself, but you don't make an ass out of me because I'm right and you're wrong."

This pretty much solidified my C in the class. The really sad part was since I had taken the class over summer school, the class was pass/fail anyways. It didn't matter whether I got a C or an A.

My senior year I took an art class.

pg.110

On the second day of the class we were making sketches of various objects. I used my thumb to smudge my pencil mark in order to create shading (a technique which I still use till this day when drawing). The instructor came up to me and in a snooty voice said,

"Excuse me, we do not smudge in this class." I was embarrassed especially since most of the class were freshman. In my mind I had prepared a whole speech. That this is art how can there be a right and wrong way of doing things. I would go on to say how many artists in their day were not appreciated because they did things differently but today they're considered geniuses. Unfortunately she would never hear these words of wisdom because the first words to come out of my mouth were,

"Hmmmm... well that's an interesting point you make. Now let me tell you why you're wrong..."

I never got to finish because my obnoxiousness got me thrown out of the classroom. I was not permitted to rejoin until I submitted a letter of apology.

That's another fine example of me

shooting myself in the foot. I had a long
history of running my mouth off. It
amazes me I never served a day of
detention in my whole life. I guess I just
knew how far I could push things. In both
cases I still believe my position was right.
Yet the way I presented myself was
entirely wrong.

At the end of my freshman year I
found an animation course that I was
interested in taking next fall; unfortunately it was in another department. As was
my understanding at the time, there were
only two things that could prevent you
from taking a class. One, the class is full,
and two you don't have the prerequisites
to the class. Since the class had no prerequisites I thought I could sign up for
the class. The department head told me
that class was reserved for IT students
only. Well, that didn't seem to present a
problem; I could switch majors to IT, take
that course and some general education
classes then switch back to my major the
next semester. I'll admit it is underhanded
but that goes on all the time at colleges.
The IT head told me that the class was
full in the fall because they had to allow

pg.112

for a certain amount of freshman students to enter the class in the Fall. "But
that's ridiculous" I told her, "they haven't
even been registered yet, and they get
preference over me, a student who is
already paying to attend the university."
She told me that I would have to switch
majors and then wait a year before I
could take the class.

Most people would have accepted
this information and moved on, but not
me. First I went to complain to my counselor. When that did no good I complained to the Dean of Students. When
that did no good I decided to talk to the
President of the university. When I arrived
in the office of the president of the university the secretary informed me that he
is a very busy man and he usually doesn't
talk to students

"That's okay," I told her, "I'll wait."

I waited 6 hours and I never got to
speak to the president of the university. I
did however get to speak with the vice
president.

"I'm surprised the secretary didn't
ask you to leave," he said.

"She did," I replied "but I told her

pg.113

my father was on the board of directors
for the school"

"Is he?" he asked.

"No, I made it up," I said admittedly.
To which the vice president of the university laughed. (That was a trick I learned.
When your not getting what you want, just
make your dad someone important. I had
told people my dad was a judge, lawyer,
and a police officer in order to manipu-
late people into giving in to me. In reality
my dad was a stocktrader on the board
of options but that never got me anywhere.) The vice president told me he
agreed with me but there was nothing he
could do anyway.

Several friends had warned me that
one day I would run off my mouth to the
wrong person and get myself pounded. If
not I was probably going to have ulcers
or a serious heart attack by the time I
reached middle age. Fortunately it never
came to that. While I was at Columbia I
began to experience very bad stomach
pains. I was diagnosed as having IBS
(Irritated Bowl Syndrome). It's really kind
of gross so I won't go into tremendous
detail. Basically when I would get angry,

or nervous I would spend several hours on
the toilet. Who would figure a medical
problem like this would cause me to reex-
amine my personality.

It took a while before I was able to
curb my temper. It's true what they say;
it's a lot easier to find fault in other people than in yourself. For example, there
was a guy in one of my computer classes
that always had something to say. Every
3 minutes his hand would go up. He
would correct the teacher during lectures
on the most minuscule details. No one in
the class could stand him. A thought
occurred to me. I do the same thing in
classes except to a much lesser degree.

The point is this; I had to learn
which battles were worth fighting.
Unfortunately some times you have to
make some noise when the situation calls
for it. If you don't you become a human
door mat. With, all the little insignificant
things that life throws at you, you have
to learn to let them slide by. Otherwise
when a big problem occurs you will not
have the energy to handle it. That's my
advice, take it or leave it, but should you
choose to take it I promise you will have

a much happier and healthier life.

Laugh, and the world laughs
with you;
Weep, and you weep alone;
For the sad old earth must
borrow its mirth,
But has trouble enough of its
own.

-Solitude , by Ella Wheeler Wilcox (1855-
1919)

I'm Not Happy,
Unless I Am
Depressed

If you read my prologue you might
have noted that I said that it is okay to
be sad when a major life changing event
happens to you. Having yourself or a family member become ill, death in the family, losing a job, or filing for a divorce are
all events that might cause someone to
become depressed. It is normal to be

depressed in these situations. It may take
you a few days, a few weeks, or even a
few months to cope with the life-chang-
ing situation. When depression seems to
linger on for more than a few months
without relief than you would be suffering
from serious prolonged depression.
Depressive disorders affect approximately
18.8 million Americans a year.

People often look at depressed people and ask, "Why is she depressed? She
has a nice home, beautiful family, great
job. She has everything; what on earth
does she have reason to be depressed ."
That is the difference between chronic
depression and temporary depression.
Temporary depression is usually caused
by an event, where lifelong depression is
caused by a chemical imbalance. A person
with lifelong depression may be
depressed for no reason at all. There
have been many studies done to try and
figure out the source of this chemical
imbalance. There have been studies done
that have tried to link depression to
everything from preservatives in our food
to chemicals added to our water. So far
all studies have been inconclusive.

pg.118

Mental illnesses are often not given the same level of urgency as other illnesses. Mental illnesses often go untreated because people are ashamed or too embarrassed to seek help. Psychologists are often referred to in this country as "shrinks''. Years ago people had to keep secret the fact that they were seeing a psychologist or they would be labeled as "crazy". Statistics show that industrialized countries have a larger presence of depression than non-industrialized countries. Here's my theory. I think industrialized countries have a larger population of depressed people simply because people are too busy to listen to their problems. If you think about it that is exactly what you pay a psychologist to do. People often think psychologists advise you on how to fix problems in your life. That, however, is not what a psychologist's function is. Psychologists help you to solve your own problems. Most of all they sit and listen. If you think about it, how many of your friends would have the time or patience to listen to you talk for an hour straight about problems in your life.

Depression is the most useless of all

the human emotions. I say this because
depression does not inspire any action.
On the contrary, depression makes one
apathetic. You feel tired and weak. You
don't feel like getting out of bed in the
morning to face the day. Any other
human emotions can be useful emotions
depending upon how you choose to act
on them. If I am envious of another person's wealth or goods, I might use that
emotion to work harder to achieve the
same. Anger is a very useful emotion.
Take for example the story of Candy
Lightner. In 1980 a drunk driver killed
Candy's 13 yr old daughter. Candy started the organization MADD (Mother's
Against Drunk Drivers) and helped raise
public awareness of the problem of drunk
driving. History is full of people who have
gotten pissed off and used their anger to
help bring about positive change. Think
about how different our country would
have been if the founding fathers of our
country had not gotten enraged with the
British. I imagine it would have gone
something like this:

     Thomas Jefferson: "John, Ben,
Alex, George, you're not going to believe

this. The British have raised the taxes on tea again."

John Hancock: "I see Tom, and how does that make you feel?"

Thomas Jefferson: "I am so depressed"

Alexander Hamilton: "Sounds like someone could use a hug."

John Hancock
Thomas Jefferson
Benjamin Franklin: "What?"
George Washington

Alexander Hamilton: "Hey, I was just trying to help."

George Washington: "You know when I get depressed I have Martha pour me a nice tall glass of Sam Adams. Sam Adams you know the name, now, you will love the taste."

Benjamin Franklin: "I am so sad I think I'll go fly a kite in the rain."

Sure, I could have made Hand Cock the flamboyantly gay one of the group but that would have been too easy. I don't know about you, but I wouldn't be quite so proud to be an American if that was a true story of the founding fathers. The point is with anger you can take that

energy and put it to something useful like
lifting weights, punching a punching bag,
jogging or running or bring about positive
change to an issue that upsets you.
Depression, after all is anger directed
inward instead of outward.

"Well, gee Brad, That's all great but
your not a Social Worker or Psychologist.
What makes you an expert on the topic
of depression?"

"Thank you for asking such a deep
thought provoking question reader." You
are right I'm not a licensed Psychologist,
however in addition to all my other problems. I have suffered from depression
from the time I was in elementary school.
I can tell you first hand it is a horrible
energy draining disease. It affects your
social life, your work life, as well as your
ability to concentrate. It clouds your
judgment and perception of everyday life.
It makes the world appear to be a much
darker place. It can even lead to more
serious mental diseases such as eating
disorders, drug abuse, alcohol abuse, and
even suicide.

If you have never suffered from
lifetime depression yourself I can closely

pg.122

relate it to alcoholism. When you are
labeled an alcoholic, even after you have
gone through all the steps of AA
(Alcoholics Anonymous) they do not say
you are cured. What they call you is a
recovering alcoholic. The difference
between being cured and being a recovering alcoholic, is recovering alcoholics
can't drink again. If they do they will
revert to their alcoholic tendencies. With
depression it is very similar. You may be
medicated and have your depression
under control but it is always there waiting for an upsetting event so it can
regain control of your mind again. When I
was younger the thing that most
depressed me was I didn't have a lot of
friends. Consequently I grew depressed
and my depression prevented me from
making new friends. It was a catch 22. I
new that if the loop was to ever break I
would have to be the one to break it. It
didn't happen over-night, in fact I still
struggle with this issue today.

Intellectual Snob And Tying It All Together

As this is the last chapter in my book, I'd first like to take the opportunity to thank you for taking the time to read my autobiography. I know there are other books about people who have led greater lives than mine and the fact that you chose to spend time reading my book instead of theirs means a lot to me. If I was able to offer you some insight on your own condition or in dealing with a friend or loved ones condition then writing this book served a significant purpose. I hope you have found some of the stories humorous and some of them moving or sad. I further hope you found the humorous stories humorous and the sad stories sad. For if you found the sad stories humorous and the humorous stories sad, that wouldn't say much for my writing abilities. That would make me sad and that wouldn't be humorous. (Forgive my ranting)

Now comes the point in the book when the author is supposed to seamlessly tie all the preceding chapters together. A good author will be able to summarize the whole entire book without your knowledge that he or she is even doing it, like some terrific magic trick. So far be it for me to deviate from the status quo. However tying together such a wide variety of subjects is no easy undertaking, but I will give it my best shot. (Notice there is nothing up my sleeve)

Even though my book touched on a variety of broad subjects there is a com-

pg.125

mon theme among almost every chapter.
If you look closely, you will notice that in
almost every chapter I speak of issues
I've had with certain people or groups of
people. This is because people are the
biggest obstacles in a physically or mentally challenged individuals life. We face
mobility obstacles, we face legal obstacles, we face environmental obstacles, we
face learning obstacles, we face equal
opportunity obstacles, and we face medical obstacles and financial obstacles all
of which are substantial. Nevertheless, it
is people who pose the biggest obstacle
to the mentally and physically handicapped. People whose attitudes lend
them to not only an unwillingness to help
but in addition frequently make our lives
more difficult then necessary. Instead of
calling this book "When Life Gives You
Lemons, Add Tequila And Salt", I could
have simply called it "Sometimes People
Suck ASS!!!!" .

    Several months ago I was talking
with one of my occupational therapists
and I referred to a third party, who was
not in the room at the time. The words I
used to describe this woman were

"Dumber than dirt". My therapist laughed, and then told me I was an "Intellectual Snob". Yes, it is true I am an "Intellectual Snob". You might think that a strange thing to admit or feel pride in but I do not. People judge each other on all sorts of superficialities. People judge people by what they look like, what kind of car they drive, how much money they make, what kind of job they hold, how much they weigh, what school they went too, who their friends with, and who their families are. I say, fuck that, as long as the person is not a moron they are okay in my book. I am not talking about intelligence in terms of how much knowledge a person possesses. I am speaking of "common sense". A misnomer if you ask me, because if common sense were, "common" you'd think more people would have it. Just the other day I was driving and an ambulance appeared behind us with sirens blaring and lights blazing. All of the vehicles including the one I was in pulled over to the side of the road to let the ambulance pass except for one car. Aside from being illegal in most states and morally wrong, it is stupid. What is the message

that person is saying? "Gee, I know the
person in the ambulance behind me might
be critically injured and in need of medical
attention but am I in a rush and don't
really hold any value for that persons
life." Maybe he or she didn't pull over
because they were late for work, a doctor's appointment, or just trying to make
the early bird special at the local deli.
Doesn't really matter. Either that person
was inconsiderate, stupid or both.
Regardless that person is beneath me.
From my first grade teacher, to the lady
at the DMV, to the people who wouldn't
lend me their phone when I got maced, to
the students in my dormitory, to the men
and women who give me a hard time
every time I try to enter an establishment
with my service dog, to the lady that
complained "Handicapped people get all
the best parking spots", they are all
beneath me intellectually; Every single
one of them. Doesn't matter what they
score on an IQ test. They are not my
intellectual equals. It is them who are the
problem and not I. I always assumed if
one person treats you like crap it is
because they are ignorant, but if a lot of

pg.128

people treat you like crap, there must be something wrong with you. It is not so. The average American adult is a moron, too caught up in the daily rituals of their problem free mundane lives.

Throughout my life I've heard phrases like this: "I feel uncomfortable around handicapped people. I never know how to act, or what to say." If this characterizes how you feel, play close attention to the next following few paragraphs.

First of all if you are looking for a general rule on how to act or what to say, I suggest you look no further than the "golden rule". For those of you who are not familiar with the "golden rule" allow me to define it for you now. "Treat other people as you would like to be treated if you were in their place."

I can't stand when people are presumptuous. They assume because I walk funny and have a speech problem that I am unintelligent. They speak to me slowly and use "small" words. Sometimes if I am with a friend or family member they will refer to me in third person as if I wasn't there. For example "and what will he have to drink, instead of asking me directly".

They speak to me in a patronizing matter like they're speaking to a child or someone who just escaped from Bellevue mental hospital. When I was growing up one of my childhood friend's mother used to speak to me in exactly such a matter after I had brain surgery. I will spell this out phonetically since I can't imitate her voice on paper.

"HeeellllOO Braaad, aaand Hoow Arre Youuuu?"

Even though I'd answer her in a normal manner, it never seemed to click that I was mentally able to comprehend normal speech. So eventually I started answering her back the same way.

"Iii ammm fiiineee, Hoow Arre Youuu?"

Five-minute conversations took fifteen minutes up to a half hour. I have had waitresses who grabbed my knife and started cutting my food for me, because they didn't think I was capable of doing it myself. Good rules of thumb, if you see a disabled person in need of assistance, ask before you try and help.

Occasionally without intention, individuals will say something asinine and

pg.130

insensitive in an attempt to draw some
connection to me. These are commonly
referred to as faux pas. For example
when I was growing up one of my classmates came up to me and said:

"Hey Brad, I broke my leg playing
soccer and had to go to the hospital.
Now I know how you must have felt."

"Really, let me ask you a question.
How long were you in the hospital for?"

"I don't know, a few hours."

"Oh, cause when I had brain surgery
I was there a few months. Few hours, few
months, yeah that's the same thing.

When I was 13 the "Make A Wish
Foundation" paid for my family and I to
go to Hawaii. All my friends of course
knew about it. Word traveled around,
and as always happens in school; soon a
hundred people know your business. One
of my peers approached me and said:

"Hey Brad, do you think if I threw
myself in front of a moving bus "Make A
Wish" would pay for me to go to Hawaii?"

"I don't know why don't you try it
and see."

These pathetic attempts to show
sympathy actually minimize the struggles

pg.131

of the handicapped rather than showing
an appreciation for it. Adults do it as
much as children.

In the opening of my book there is
a quote from the movie "City Slickers". In
that scene Billy Crystal's character
"Mitch" is asking Jack Palance's character
"Curly", what the secret to life is. Curly
answers back "One Thing". That is why I
say if you can find something to do that
you enjoy, that makes your whole life
better. It will not fix the physical or emotional pain and it certainly won't stop the
longing to be normal again, but it dis-
tracts you from the problem so you can
enjoy life to a greater degree.

You may guess by my title for this
book that I did my fair share of drinking.
In the opening paragraph I urge the reader not to drink their problems away.
When I took health in High School, my
health book said the worst kind of
drinkers are problem drinkers. I don't
know if I agree with that, I happen to
think the worst kind of drinker is an abu-
sive alcoholic. So if you have the occa-
sional drink to forget about your problems, what is wrong with that? I am not

suggesting you go out on a binge, but a
few drinks on a Friday or Saturday night
might help you alleviate some of the
stresses that life presents you. A psychologist might suggest you take a
much-needed vacation to help in alleviat-
ing stress. I disagree, because when you
get back all your problems will be waiting
for you. It is not a long-term solution. I'd
say anything that gets your mind off your
disability; as long as it is not hurting you
or anyone else and is not illegal is a good
thing.

Growing up I would visit both sets of
grandparents in retirement communities.
When I got older I volunteered at the
nursing home to fulfill my community
service requirement. The senior citizens
would gather in one room to play cards,
rummy cube, watch T.V, and socialize.
Yet there was always one group that
seemed to separate themselves from the
rest. They would sit in their chairs and
wait as if for a bus. I began to wonder
what are they waiting for? Then it came
to me, they're waiting to die. Their
friends might have died, maybe their
spouses as well. Perhaps their children

pg.133

don't come to visit them that often. For whatever the reason, they have lost the will to live and are waiting for their life to end. They don't have that "One Thing" that Jack Palance's character Curly was talking about.

There are a select few people who are lucky. They can go their whole lives without ever having to deal with a major tragedy to themselves or to their loved ones. They can sympathize with their friends who have issues, but they can never fully comprehend their struggles. However for everyone else who has to deal with the sour lemons that fate throws at us, we need Tequila and salt to help keep the unpleasant taste down

Dedications

I'd first like to dedicate this book to my parents. For pushing me farther ahead than I ever
thought I was capable of. For believing in me even
when I didn't believe in myself. Lastly for supporting
me through all life's trial and tribulations.

My family and friends who suggested I write
this book in the first place and sticking by me.

My dog Liza you'll never know how many ways
you've saved me. You're the best dog ever.

Lastly I'd like to thank all the people who have
been a pain in my ass in my life. Without you I
would not had stories to put in this book. Also
those who told me over and over again what I was
not capable of. You provided me with enough spite
to prove you wrong.

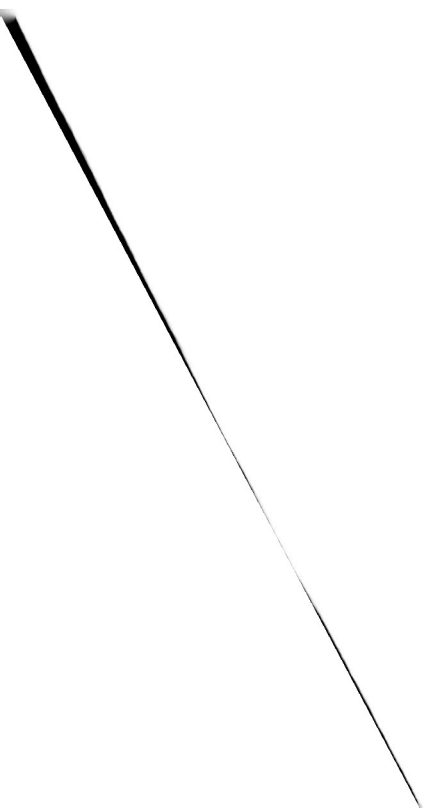

* 9 7 8 0 6 1 5 1 6 0 4 8 1 *